W9-AQO-817

Mondo DC

An Insider's Guide to Washington, DC's Most Unusual Tourist Attractions

By

Jeff Bagato

PANIC
RESEARCH
PRP PRESS

© 2005 Jeff Bagato. All Rights Reserved.

No part of this book may be reproduced, stored in a retrieval system, or transmitted by any means without the written permission of the author.

First published by AuthorHouse 04/07/05

ISBN: 1-4208-2138-5 (sc)

Library of Congress Control Number: 2004097680

Printed in the United States of America
Bloomington, Indiana

This book is printed on acid-free paper.

These articles represent the views and experiences of the author, and do not constitute a warranty or assumption of liability of any kind. Due to the changeability of contact information (hours, costs, websites, etc), the author cannot guarantee the accuracy of this information. Please contact the sites directly for up-to-date information. The author welcomes reader feedback on information changes and their experiences visiting these sites.

Library cataloging data
Title: Mondo DC: An Insider's Guide to Washington, DC's Most Unusual Tourist Attractions

Author: Jeff Bagato

Publisher: Panic Research Press, P.O. Box 2482, Merrifield, VA 22116
Includes photographs by the author

Keywords: Tour Guides; Washington, DC (Metropolitan Area); Roadside Attractions; Little Museums; Folk Art; History

Panic Research Agency
Panic Research Press
P.O. Box 2482
Merrifield, VA 22116

www.panicresearch.com
www.mondoDC.com

authorHOUSE™

1663 LIBERTY DRIVE, SUITE 200
BLOOMINGTON, INDIANA 47403
(800) 839-8640
WWW.AUTHORHOUSE.COM

Acknowledgments

I'd like to thank Vicki Wawrzyniec and Tom and Angie Scanlan, for their helpful first reading; Mia and Henry, for support and travel companionship above and beyond the call of a family unit; and especially everyone who shared their artifacts, archives, museums, homes, and stories with me. I'd also like to thank Mr. Dixie for agreeing to pose as the cover star.

Some of these chapters appeared in different and abridged form in the following publications: *The Washington Post, Washington Post Magazine, Washington Post Weekend, Washington City Paper*, and *Bizarre* (UK).

Table of Contents

Welcome to Mondo DC!

Watcha gonna see next? A real castle built from scratch by a monomaniac's bare hands? The "Indian shooting buffaloes" painting that hangs on a Merrifield, Virginia, auto body shop? The tin man costume from Broadway's "The Wiz"? A portrait of former Vice President Spiro Agnew dressed as a clown? How about opium pipes, real corpses as anatomical models, tiny trees, or tinier zoos? Would you like to type on an old World War II encoding machine once used by real spies? Hunt for ghosts on Alexandria's King Street, or for monsters in a cathedral? Descend into Roman catacombs without leaving town? Research assassinations, hang out with anarchists, or gape at pin up art?

From the curious to the cultured, the offbeat to the obscure, the Washington, DC, metropolitan area is blessed with many amazing places offering magical journeys and visions. **Mondo DC** is your private guide to discovering the region's secret spots often overlooked by standard tour books—little museums, odd archives, hidden monuments, unusual tours, roadside art, and even esoterica. What unites them is a special feeling of uniqueness. Or strangeness. Or obscurity. In any case, the feeling of specialness increases the closer you get. And **Mondo DC** gives you an unprecedented insider's view of these attractions, revealing fascinating stories about their history, founders, and collections that even many longtime Washingtonians don't know.

The smaller operations are labors of love, determined to highlight forgotten cultural activities. Often volunteer run, their hours sometimes are restricted or by appointment only. The larger ones house unusually specialized collections, or a particularly rare and fascinating specimen. The best part? Most are free or low cost. For your convenience, I've included contact information, hours, and costs. (As this information can change unpredictably, it's best to call or check websites to verify it.)

Of course, local treasures like the Smithsonian (the largest museum complex in the world), the National Zoo, the U.S. Holocaust Memorial Museum, U.S. Botanic Garden, and the National Aquarium (among others) are chock full of fascinating stuff. These places haven't been included here (unless they have something truly bizarre) because they appear in standard guides to the area. Nor does this book list restaurants, nightclubs, hotels, or other amenities essential for travelers. Look to more conventional guides for that information.

A quick note on the title. **Mondo DC** refers to the genre of film documentaries started by Gualtiero Jacopetti's *Mondo Cane* in 1962. A montage of odd human and animal behavior from around the world, *Mondo Cane* (translated from the Italian as "World Gone to the Dogs") is a bit like a cinematic *Ripley's Believe it or Not*. This "shockumentary" spawned a rash of imitators over the following decades, starting with Jacopetti's own *Mondo Cane 2*, and including *Mondo Infame*, *Mondo Bizarro*, *Wild Wild World*, *Mondo Topless*, and *Mondo New York*. By focusing on the history of the quirkiest places in the Washington area, **Mondo DC** aims to be as amusing, informative, and stimulating as the best of the Mondo movies.

I'll be posting updates to this book and new discoveries on the web at **www.MondoDC.com**. If you've discovered a Mondo site in the DC area, please let me know. I'm always up for touring!

There are so many great, offbeat places in the Washington, DC, area that you can visit. How many have you seen? Do you know where you're going?

Tourists, start your engines. Your trip through **Mondo DC** is about to begin!

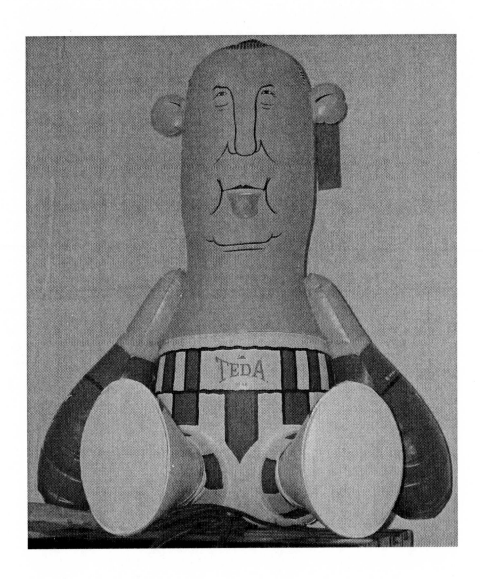

The Agnew Room

Hornbake Library
University of Maryland
College Park, MD
(301) 405-9058
Website: www.lib.umd.edu/ARCV/info.html
Hours: M-F 10 a.m.-5 p.m.; W 5-8 p.m.; Sat 12-5 p.m.
Cost: Free

Every celebrity deserves a portrait of themselves as a clown. A man named Baruta certainly thought Vice President Spiro T. Agnew deserved this honor, so in 1969 he broke out his oil paints and got to work. The artist perfectly captured Agnew's large nose, prominent forehead, and squinted eyes, then dressed him up in a black top hat, a tie, and a raggedy black jacket. Agnew the Clown's face make-up is classic white greasepaint accented by a reddened nose and big eyebrows. Tufts of orange hair poke out from under the hat brim. His head is tilted slightly to the right, his mouth set in an ambiguous straight line that vaguely suggests mirth—or lips tightened on a dirty secret. Some might say no one deserves such tribute more than Spiro Agnew, but there's no record of whether Mr. Baruta intended his work as satire.

Simply titled "Vice President Spiro T. Agnew as a Clown," the painting now resides in the Agnew Room, a glass-walled repository of memorabilia gifted to our nation's thirty-ninth Vice President back when he served as Nixon's second in command. There are about twenty-five other paintings here, plus two carved wooden objects believed to be African birthing chairs (disassembled), branding irons bearing the initials "STA," a foot high cement monogram of the same initials highlighted in small tiles, a blowup caricature doll shaped like Agnew wearing boxing gloves, and a cape made of monkey fur. A cross between a garage sale and an exhibit of folk art, the collection answers the question, "What do you give a man who has everything except, uh, the presidency?"

Set deep in the Hornbake Library, the central facility for special collections on the University of Maryland's College Park Campus, the Agnew Room comprises the minor part (you knew that) of the man's vice presidential papers deposited here in 1974, shortly after his resignation. "There are 406 linear feet of material, a couple hundred boxes," notes Jennie Levine, Curator for Historical Manuscripts at the library. "That doesn't include memorabilia or the stuff received from the Agnew family in the mid-90s, which is probably 200 to 300 feet of material." These files allow researchers to plumb the depths of Agnew's vice presidential legacy, from his support for the space program to his "nattering nabobs of negativism" speech, which characterized his critical view of the media. In between the paperwork, Agnew made time to receive state visitors bearing zebra skins, monogrammed golf supplies, fancy ice pitchers, fine china, and other loot. All of these slipped into the Hornbake Library with the historical documents. [You can take a virtual tour of the collection, including photos of some memorabilia, on the library's website: www. newsdesk.umd.edu/sociss/release.cfm?ArticleID=815.]

Before joining the archival staff four years ago, Levine worked on the catalog to these papers as a grad student, but it didn't ruin her enthusiasm for the collection. She relishes showing off the oddities, pointing out highlights and personal favorites, and offering delightful tidbits about them. As we walk through the room, she pulls out a homemade golf club— a giant driver attached to a metal pole with electrical tape. Above his signature, the maker, James Penatzer, wrote on it in white ink: "Presented to Vice President Spiro Agnew/For Safety of the American People."

"Agnew was a big golfer," Levine notes. "Admirers often sent him golf-themed stuff. We have golf bags, golf balls, all kinds of things. [Penatzer's gift] looks like it was made out of papier mache."

She's also pleased to point out another amateur painting of Agnew that the conservators have taken to calling "Beaver Teeth." You'll have to look closely at this competent likeness to notice that Agnew's teeth are visibly stained with a brown pigment. Another portrait, this one by a Pennsylvania high school student, shows Agnew in a blue suit and patriotic red, white, and blue tie; more unusually, a large red and white aura circles his head. Levine also happily points out a caricature of Agnew heading for Washington; the cartoon was signed by his classmates from Forrester High School's (in Baltimore) Class of '37. The weirdest portrait, however, is so lifelike it's uncanny, particularly since it's constructed entirely of feathers. This gift from Indonesia's former President Suharto might also be considered a political commentary. Any of these pictures would make a remarkable find for a connoisseur of thrift store art.

If you're not in the art market, then there's plenty of other junk, I mean, artifacts to see. "This is one of my favorites, this green thing," Levine says, pointing to a squat urn-like object on a top shelf. "It's an ice chest from Asia. I know that because my father has one just like it that he got in Southeast Asia in the 1970s." Presumably made of cast iron and set with designs that look Cambodian, Agnew acquired the thing on a goodwill tour, possibly the same one that yielded the light-up folding screen from China, and the old-fashioned chafing dish from Iran. "He traveled around and was our ambassador," Levine says. "It was his job to travel and represent the United States."

If those things aren't odd enough for you, there's plenty more. Try the inflatable Agnew doll wearing boxing trunks and gloves. Smells like satire to me, marketing a punching dummy to the press corps and other "radical liberals" (a term first used by Agnew) who may have wanted to take a swing at the Republican gadfly who baited them with quirky, alliterative phrases like "nattering nabobs" and "hopeless, hysterical hypochondriacs of history."

Remember the Agnew watch? This novelty item from the early 1970s featured a caricature of the veep wearing stars 'n' bars shorts and shoes, his arms pointing out the time. It was marketed by the Dirty Time Company using the tag line: "What kind of wrist watch does Mickey Mouse wear? A Spiro Agnew watch." One Agnew admirer must have felt that if he was wearing an Agnew watch, then Agnew should wear a watch with his likeness—so he made one. The Agnew Room has it, of course. This homemade timepiece has an inch-and-a-half thick red naugahyde band and a large dial embellished with a hand-drawn Uncle Sam whose face is a photograph of a man with large glasses. Writing near the image identifies the man as "L.J.B.: Man of the Hour." [Not to be confused with LBJ.] The watch is mounted on a velvet-covered board and has a gilt wood frame. Talk about your lifetime achievements!

My personal favorites are three pieces of folk art. One is a silver robot cleverly pieced together from metal odds and ends, like drill bits, springs, egg beaters, bolts, and other shiny things. It stands about a foot high on a base with two pen holders and a plaque that says, "Vice President Spiro T. Agnew." The artist is unknown. The most disturbing object in the whole collection sits on a file cabinet out in the workroom; this marble bust portrays Nixon and Agnew as Siamese twins that share the same cranium. Nixon faces right, Agnew left; an eagle rests at each of their necks, and the Capitol stands between them.

The most primitive of these three artworks would go well in Baltimore's American Visionary Art Museum. It's a wooden cage, made using dowels for bars, containing a weird, wooden, fish-like creature with one eye made of a golf ball and the other a large marble. The cage is painted blue and decorated with phrases cut from magazines that clearly send a message of adoration and encouragement. "How Can You Tell," reads one piece glued on the top of the cage; next, "Follow the leader," "High Noon," and "For You." On one side, the clipping reads, "Maybe what you've got isn't ordinary." The other side bears the message, "How to shave ten strokes

5

off your game." Next to a thin strip of animal fur, a label made from a piece of flexible white plastic is tied to the top of the box; this identifies the maker as "dupuis [sic], Port Arthur, TX." On the bottom of the box, there's a mailing address and canceled stamps. This golf totem isn't just a marvelous work of outsider art—it's also mail art!

Agnew's big score, as far as state gifts are concerned, has to be that full-length monkey fur cape. The gift of Kenyan dignitaries visiting in 1971, the cape features huge epaulets tufted with long white fur. In a photograph documenting the occasion, a fur-wrapped Agnew sports a huge grin while the Kenyans adjust the fit. Levine reveals that one male archivist once wore the cape, a fleeting romp for which he requests anonymity. Levine herself is reluctant to handle it, mostly because it may have been treated with DDT. "That's the rumor," she says. "Someone who had a conservation background said that at the time that was the custom, to have these things treated to kill germs."

Levine once came across a second pelt in the collection, this one from a zebra (though not fashioned into a garment). "I'd prefer to never touch that again," she laughs. But don't be shy should you want to see these items yourself, Levine is quick to add. She'll happily bring them—or any of the deposit's eccentric wonders, for that matter—down to the Reading Room, the customary place for visitors to examine special collections. [Sorry, private tours of the Agnew Room aren't available.]

Spiro Theodore Agnew was a Baltimore boy, a biographical fact that almost guarantees notoriety. (You've heard of John Waters, right?) He was born in the city in 1918, got a law degree from the University of Baltimore, and became chief executive of Baltimore County, Maryland, in 1966. He jumped from there to the state governor's mansion, serving from 1966 until 1968, when Richard Nixon picked him to be his running mate. Shortly after the Nixon/Agnew reelection in 1972, the U.S. Attorney in Baltimore began investigating the veep for irregularities in contributions to his gubernatorial campaign. Agnew resigned from office on October 10, 1973. Charged with tax evasion, he pleaded "no contest," but it didn't help: He was fined $10,000 and given three years' probation. Agnew was only the second Vice President to resign from office, and the first to do so while facing criminal charges. He died in 1996, and was buried in Timonium, Maryland.

It's not unusual for a vice president to retain possession of objects received while in office, even though presidents technically don't own official gifts. "The rules for what a vice president gets to keep and what the president gets to keep are different," Levine explains, "and the rules were different back then." Levine's not sure why the University of Maryland was lucky enough to receive the deposit—Agnew's papers are a particularly prized possession, even if the monkey fur cape is, well, less welcome— although it certainly has to do with Agnew's lifelong attachment to his home state and the school's long-running archival program. At least one other likely repository for the goods—the Nixon Presidential Library—has yet to be constructed. Nixon's own papers, Levine points out, are housed in the National Archives, having been confiscated during the Watergate trials.

Agnew's papers opened to the public in 1998, the year the archivists finished cataloging them. Prior to that, Levine says, "a portion of them opened when he was still alive. There was a big ceremony in 1995 that Agnew was present for." The catalog doesn't really account for the memorabilia, however. "We're not quite sure what to do with it," Levine admits. "I'm sure we'll figure it out, but it hasn't been a priority. The emphasis has been on the papers."

Take the boxes of souvenir tie clips—hundreds of them!—printed with Agnew's official signature. What would you do with these leftovers? Levine has hit on a novel solution. "I could almost promise every visitor a tie clip," she says. "I'm happy to give away a Spiro T. Agnew tie clip to anyone who wants."

The cape, the clown, and a free clip to boot. That's gotta be an offer you can't refuse.

Alexandria Ghost and Graveyard Tour

meets at Ramsay House Visitor's Centre
221 King St.
Alexandria, VA
(703) 519-1749
Website: www.alexcolonialtours.com
Hours: Fri & Sat 7:30 & 9 p.m.; Wed, Thurs & Sun 7:30 p.m.,
April through November
Cost: Adults: $7; children: $5

Have you heard the one about Alexandria's Burning Bride? Sometimes children see her—a sad young woman in a long white gown—when their parents take them into the Christmas Attic's House in the Country boutique, on the corner of Fairfax and King Streets in Old Town Alexandria. Perhaps the kids are just bored hanging out in a store full of delicate Christmas trinkets they can't touch. But adults have seen her too—and heard her cries and moans as she scrabbles at the mysteriously jammed lock of the upstairs room where she was trapped 135 years ago, after she dropped her kerosene lantern and caught herself on fire...

As Wellington Watts spins the tale of young Laura Shaefer, one of many relics of the eighteenth and nineteenth centuries still standing in this old colonial port city, the thirty people grouped around him begin to drift back in time. It's an easy journey to make as night descends around us, although Watts is the only one of us dressed for the colonial age. From tricorn hat to buckled shoes, with his knee-length breeches, puffy-sleeved white shirt, and buttoned vest, our tour guide is prepared to meet the phantoms of Old Town in the style to which they were accustomed. (The ladies conduct tours wearing plain maid's dresses and little white cloth caps.) Watts' enthusiasm for his subject matter flows over us as easily as his booming voice, pulling us deeper into the past, a candlelit lantern held high to light the way. The roar of the motorcycles on King Street begins to seem very far away.

As we stroll a six block circle starting at the Ramsay House, now a visitor's center at 221 King Street, we pass the former homes of the Ramsays, Fairfaxes, and Carlyles, prosperous merchants and members in good-standing of the highest social class. Their names figure prominently in the history of our country, but as one might expect, they've left a few skeletons in their closets, walls, and cellars. Ghosts are everywhere down here near the Potomac River—or so it's said. Like the old sea captain who keeps watch from the attic of his house on Sea Captain's row, watching for the return of his lady love, who died on the boat she took to England. The Dalton House doesn't have a ghost necessarily, just a reputation for providing nightmares to tenants of its basement apartment. Not just any nightmares, but the same three nightmares repeated for many different people over the course of two centuries. The discoveries of the modern renter who explores the clues of these three nightmares are fascinating...so much so, it would be a shame to give them away.

Alexandria's Original Ghost and Graveyard Tour introduces plenty of ghosts, and as promised on their brochure, will abandon you in a graveyard! But it's far more than a meander through the macabre moments of Virginia's oldest port city. The tour mixes true tales of hauntings and a few ghostly yarns with tidbits of the town's history and colonial customs, a city walk, and gross-out jokes. You'll learn about the haunted houses on the block of Fairfax Street between King and Cameron Streets—and why the Carlyle House in the middle has no ghosts! There's a visit to the old city morgue and a murder mystery involving pickles. And that's just the "South Tour."

The North Tour covers Gadsby's Tavern, Market Square, George Washington's townhouse, and St. Asaph Street. Gadsby's Tavern is rife with ghosts, although Washington's Old Town quarters are not. On St. Asaph, Watts doesn't cover a particular landmark. "When it comes to private homes we don't usually point out which homes are haunted," he explains, "because people have the tendency after the tour to go knock on their windows and say 'Hi, can we see your ghosts?'"

During the tour, I overhear several people commenting how much fun it is to learn about the town's history on this ghostly walk. When I report this feedback to Watts, he laughs, "I have more fun on my tour than anybody, believe me." That statement is probably more true than some of his anecdotes. An extremely animated storyteller, Watts makes colonial history a pure delight. His demonstration of the "language of the fan" is particularly rollicking. If this quaint, eighteenth century system of courtship symbols—once used by ladies to attract and deny suitors at fancy balls—suddenly makes a comeback in proms, cotillions, and discos, you'll know who's to blame once you've seen him in action. His tour patter effortlessly imparts details of the colonial customs of burial, courtship, marriage, and hygiene. If you've ever wondered why they wore powdered wigs back then, how they stored ice, or what symbol identified a hearse, you need only take the tour. In a mere hour's postprandial walk, you'll delve into the past and emerge refreshed, informed, and better acquainted with the prestigious ladies and gentlemen who lived and died along these streets—and now haunt here.

A quarter century old and counting, the Ghost and Graveyard Tour is now a part of Old Town Alexandria history itself. In June 2003, Watts bought the company, Doorways to Old Virginia, from his former bosses Ed and Stella Michaels after they retired, renaming it Alexandria Colonial Tours. Watts himself gave tours with the Michaels' company for four years. Indeed, all the Michaels' guides have stayed with Watts since the transition. "This is a big family; they love what they do," Watts reports. So you're sure to get a good tour no matter who conducts it. This changing of hands is also something of a tradition, as Stella Michaels worked as a tour guide for the company before she took it over. When she became the boss, Stella copyrighted all the stories and the ones she subsequently researched and wrote. Watts and the rest of his guides work from these licensed scripts.

How many of these anecdotes are true? Watts isn't telling, but he assures me there's truth to them all. "Our stories are based on historical fact, if not at times on hysterical fact," he quips.

When it comes to ghosts, that may be as solid an answer as you're likely to get from anybody.

Anarchy Mural

Main Reading Room
Thomas Jefferson Building
Library of Congress
101 Independence Ave, SE
Washington, DC
(202) 707-5000
Website: www.loc.gov
Hours: 10:00 a.m.-5:30 p.m. M-Sat
Cost: Free

Just a few years ago I was roaming the complicated mezzanine of the Library of Congress's Main Gallery (possibly looking for a bathroom) when I made a crucial discovery in Washington's political and art history legacy: Anarchy lives in the Library of Congress!

She greets visitors there with open arms, bare breasts, and a dripping wine cup from a semicircular painting above an elevator near the Main Reading Room. Installed in 1896, Anarchy's still dynamic, compelling, and crazy after all these years.

The power of Anarchy's image somehow made me forget all the other artwork that overwhelms the walls of this ornate shrine to learning and wisdom. On that first visit, I was only vaguely aware, too, that Anarchy herself was merely the bad end of a series of five lunettes placed around the doors of the Main Reading Room. Entitled simply "Government" after the central panel, the series briefly outlines two courses of public leadership: "Corrupt Legislation" and "Good Government." The latter appears personified as a smug and dull matron presiding over the counting of beans and voting chits with the scale of justice. Good Government's reign leads to "Peace and Prosperity," another dowdy woman who bears a strained expression and a tense posture, bracing herself as if suffering from back pain. Clearly bored with the dull, sleepy-eyed youths at her side, Peace rests in the kind of paradise the Talking Heads once described when they sang: "Heaven is a place where nothing ever happens." Her torso and breasts are bare, but her legs are chastely covered. "Corruption" seems more slothful in dress and posture than her "good" counterpart and holds a one-sided scale; in the corrupt world, "Good Government's" abundant fields of grain are replaced by smoking factory chimneys. Obviously a bad scene.

Yet "Corruption" leads to that exciting, irresistible *femme fatale* "Anarchy," who tears off her garments, wears writhing snakes in her hair, and daringly waves her wine cup in one hand while brandishing a burning scroll in the other. At her feet she tramples symbols of literature, art, religion, and law. Her irrepressible companions, Violence and Ignorance, tear apart a classical Roman edifice and dump the rubble into an abyss. Down in front with the discarded symbols of civilization there rolls a black bowling ball-type bomb—the kind Rocky and Bullwinkle's archenemy Boris Badenov carried like a calling card. Ever the mad bomber, Anarchy has lit the weapon's fuse with the flames of the torch she carries, thus sowing the seeds of her own destruction.

This rather heavy-handed allegory was rendered in 1895 by Elihu Vedder, an artist well-known in his day as an illustrator of popular greeting cards and a best-selling edition of Omar Khayyam's *Rubaiyat*. Vedder was chosen as a muralist for Bowdoin College by the architect Charles McKim, who recommended the painter when McKim headed the Library of Congress project. Final approval was made by Edward Pearce Casey, the interior designer of the library's Thomas Jefferson Building; the over-the-top ornateness of the place—with every surface either overdecorated or imposing—is Casey's doing.

Vedder drew inspiration for his "Government" figures from sculptures and paintings he saw in Rome, where he lived and worked for most of his career. Fitting the neoclassical pretensions of Washington's federal-style architecture, the figures wear togas and sandals, rest on stately marble benches built on pillars of carved urns and lions, and vote using the method of ancient democracies—tossing a chit into a vase. (No chance of mistaken chads there!) Vedder had seen William Blake's drawings during a trip to London, and the Romantic's influence can be seen in Vedder's own use of smooth, expressive outlines, heroic poses, and washes of pale color. Vedder also created the library's mosaic portrait of Minerva, the Roman goddess of learning, but the image is static, much like other works there.

Vedder considered himself a landscape painter, and he brought a precision of naturalistic detail to his visionary and allegorical work that makes it an early example of magic realism. "Lair of the Sea Serpent," a painting from 1864, portrays a Mediterranean beach delightfully contoured by dunes and shrubs. A gargantuan snake big enough to swallow a dinosaur curls languorously in the sun. The image is so realistic, one believes the beast truly belongs there. The effect repeats in "The Roc's Egg," where an enormous egg dwarfs such realistically detailed desert nomads you almost forget the egg is there. Vedder achieves similarly normalizing effects when he painted angels, medusas, the Pleiades, or "The Sphinx of the Seashore."

Any of these works might have graced the covers of a later century's pulp science fiction paperbacks.

In comparison to his realistic fantasies, Vedder's "Government" series seems a rather mundane version of an idealized classical society. However, the central panel, "Government" itself, features two androgynously beautiful angels; you can almost believe that they appeared this way, wings and all, in Vedder's studio. But as a larger-than-life figure made surprisingly vivid, "Anarchy" more closely fits the spirit of Vedder's visionary work.

Aside from being the most hedonistic figure of the series, and despite an attachment to a misunderstood political ideology that seems dangerous or juvenile to the public, Anarchy is just more fun to look at. She alone displays a delightful sense of movement, a dynamic, off-centered composition, the charm of nakedness, and expansive, abandoned gestures. But her face has a grim cast. She knows that tomorrow will bring a hangover from her present indulgences, and that some kind of reconstruction will have to begin. The power of this painting is that it suggests this character development, which removes it from the rigid allegorical structure that confines the other works of Vedder's "Government" series.

Whether an ill omen or a delight, Anarchy's residence in Washington makes sense in the company of the myriad other ambassadors, politicos, ideologues, and mad dreamers who likewise spice a stodgy bureaucratic stew.

Assassination Archives and Research Center

1003 K St., NW, Suite 204
Washington, DC
(202) 393-1921
Website: www.aarclibrary.org
Hours: By appointment only
Cost: Free

Where else but the capital of the free world would you expect to find a place with the stated mission of "acquiring, preserving and providing information on political assassinations"? Just because of its influence on world events, Washington, DC, would seem a logical home for the Assassination Archives and Research Center (AARC). But there's a more practical reason Jim Lesar—and the archive he founded and runs—is based here. Lesar specializes in Freedom of Information Act law, and most of the documents in his collection were released as a result of that legislation. That means the Assassination Archives has large holdings of intelligence materials from the FBI and CIA related to organized crime, terrorism, John Lennon's assassination, and, of course, the shooting deaths of the big three 1960s heroes: JFK, RFK, and MLK.

But this doesn't mean the archives is a hotbed of conspiracy theorizing. Lesar assures me that his clients are primarily researchers or historians, because the collection "focuses on more serious material and government documents." Walking into this unassuming office in a rundown K Street office building, my conspiratorial fever dreams of linking UFOs, Nazis, and JFK quickly dissipate upon being confronted by three crowded, cluttered rooms lined with file cabinets and piled with cartons of typescript legal papers. The Assassination Archives *should* have plenty of stuff; Lesar and co-founder Bud Fensterwald, Jr., started collecting material in 1969, and first opened the archives in 1985. According to their website, the AARC collection is not just "the largest private archives and library of its kind," it's "the most extensive collection of records on the JFK assassination in private hands."

Who needs the fictional excitement of conspiracy theories when you've got 300,000 pages of CIA records released under the JFK Act? "It's probably the most illuminating group of CIA documents ever released," Lesar tells me. "Because there are so few redactions, it's an unparalleled glimpse into the workings of the CIA." Talk about serious! You'd really have to know your stuff to even care that these reams of paper reveal the code name AMLASH, let alone key CIA stations and personnel. Should these thrills be insufficient, you can skim the 100,000 pages of FBI Headquarters files on the JFK assassination investigation—or get specific with the 40,000 card index to the files of the Dallas field office investigation. To broaden your scope, examine 80,000 pages of records the FBI made available to the House Select Committee on Assassinations, including files on organized crime figures and Cuban exile groups.

The collection doesn't stop there. Lesar's got films, photographs, unpublished manuscripts, letters, notes, periodical articles, and audiotapes. Among the 40 to 50 videotapes are TV and radio broadcasts, interviews, and film footage shot for Canadian television. There are about 2,000 books, too, covering foreign and domestic assassinations throughout history. Today, many key documents are available on-line and on CD-ROM.

And in this amazing library a single volume finally relaunches my flights of conspiratorial fancy. I've spotted Sybil Leek and Bert R. Sugar's examination of the 1963 assassinations, *The Assassination Chain*. What can this mean? Well, Leek was the author of numerous texts on astrology and witchcraft, including her best-selling autobiography, *Diary of a Witch*. Maybe everything really is connected!

The Awakening Giant

Hains Point
East Potomac Park, SW
Washington, DC
(202) 485-9880
Hours: 6 a.m.-midnight
Cost: Free

My three year old son climbs into the giant's mouth and curls up on his tongue. Older kids climb the giant's foot, left hand, and bent knee, although his outstretched right arm is too tall for most. The giant is patient, lying still while sneakers trample and kick him, hands pull his beard and fingers, and endless photos are snapped of him. If the giant stood up, he'd have a great view of the Potomac River down to Alexandria on one side and of the Mall on the other. But he's not going anywhere. All of his imaginary body and most of his limbs lie deep in the earth here at Hains Point. Only five body parts rise above the surface. Judging by the look on his face, he apparently had a rough night and isn't quite ready to meet the day. Maybe the giant seems to be roaring and thrashing because he's fighting his way out of the ground, or perhaps he could use a bit of the hair of the dog that bit him. Or maybe he knows that his stay with us is temporary, his fate uncertain.

The awakening giant may look perpetually grouchy, but as one of the most popular sculptures in town, he seldom lacks playful company. His five sandcast aluminum body parts sprawled out across the lawn form a wonderful *trompe l'oeil* artwork that sparks the imagination, conjuring images of Gulliver in Lilliput, or Abe Lincoln come down from his monument to lay on the grass. To many Buddhists, the emerging giant symbolizes the human awakening from the imprisonment of material concerns. He could also be Jack's beanstalk giant, who landed hard when the plant was axed (another reason for the giant's grimace). One of the few playful public sculptures in Washington, "The Awakening" makes a great diversion from the nearby monument core.

The giant has been a District resident since 1980, when the Eleventh International Sculpture Conference scattered 500 sculptures throughout the city. "The Awakening" was the only one of those artworks to stay, mostly because its maker, J. Seward Johnson, Jr., placed it on permanent loan to the U.S. Department of the Interior, which owns the land. The sculpture has been available for purchase from the beginning, but according to Glen

Demarr, Project Manager at the Park Service, there are no plans to purchase the giant for the site. Not many people know that Johnson is willing to give it away. His curator Paula Stoeke tells me, "There's an ongoing offer to gift it to the city if that location is available."

An heir to the Johnson & Johnson pharmaceutical fortune (think Band-Aids and baby shampoo), Johnson has made a career creating hyperrealistic public sculptures of city dwellers doing simple, normal things like sitting under a tree, reading a newspaper, skateboarding, talking, or hailing a cab. In creating "The Awakening," Johnson broke his own mold, so to speak, by playing tricks with scale to create an immediately recognizable fantasy.

Most of the giant's interactions with the public have been pleasant ones, but he has had some run-ins with automobiles that would have been fatal for his guests and playmates. Over the years, his hand, head, and outstretched arm have been damaged. All three accidents resulted from motorists taking a nearby hairpin turn too fast. In each case, Johnson made the necessary repairs. For a short time, the giant's face went back to the sculptor's Princeton, New Jersey, studio for work, and the statue had to do without.

Although the sculpture could be bought and relocated at any time, the most serious threat to the giant's Washington residency is the National Peace Garden planned for his Hains Point home turf. Congress first authorized such a monument in 1987 and has extended that mandate while the foundation to construct the memorial raises funds for its design. The giant lives in DC in a kind of limbo—at any time he could be bought or displaced. Johnson would like to see him stay.

"We are very interested in keeping the giant on Hains Point because of the city's international visitors," Stoeke says. "The artist loves to know the sculpture is being seen by people from all parts of the world. I hear many of the tour buses take the Hains Point Loop just to see the giant. Since this is such a large scale sculpture, he really needs room to sprawl, and this particular site has been ideal."

A permanent home in Washington—even though taxed without representation—would surely make the awakening giant live happily ever after.

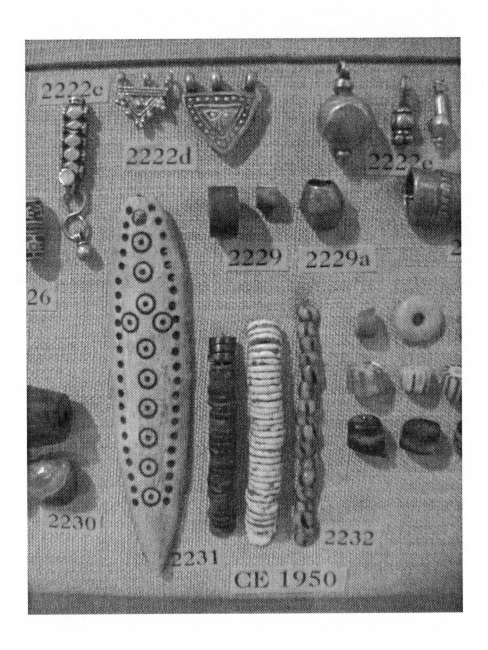

Bead Museum

The Jenifer Building
400 Seventh St., NW, Ground Floor
Washington, DC
(202) 624-4500
Website: www.beadmuseumdc.org
Hours: W-Sat 11 a.m.-4 p.m.; Sun. 1-4 p.m.
Cost: Free

What do you know about beads? Are they merely the plastic baubles kids use to make charm bracelets and keychains, or bits of pearl or metal found in jewelry, or miniature works of art that speak volumes about cultural traditions and technological development? That's right, it's a trick question. Beads can be all of these and much more—and have been for a long, long time.

Just check out the "Bead Timeline of History," the Bead Museum's "centerpiece exhibition" (and its only permanent one). Starting with a cluster of Sumerian shell beads at least 10,000 years old, the timeline extends to the present day in the span of thirty-five feet, covering major cultures around the globe. Ancient Egypt, Rome, China, Korea, France... well, you get the idea. The wide array of colors, shapes, and materials represented in these tiny objects (most are smaller than a quarter) makes a feast for the eyes. Oddities pop out as you scan the display cases: animals carved from bone or formed in gold, little Sumerian heads that might be made of Sculpey but are actually formed from glass, doll-sized urns, six tiny fists made of bluish faience, fanciful blown glass shapes, elaborately patterned millefiori glass beads, and so on.

One of the most unusual beads is #508, listed in the timeline's thick catalog as a "typical Phoenician 'demon' pendant." This creature is not nearly as terrifying as it sounds. With its large round eyes and pointed nose, the "demon" looks most like that fearsome beast, the lemur. "All of the head pendants on the Timeline date from the 7th to the 3rd to 2nd centuries BCE, and the demon masks are among the earlier examples," notes Jim Lankton, via email from London. As the author of *A Bead Timeline* (the catalog to the exhibit, available in the Bead Museum's gift shop), and the donor of many of the timeline beads, Lankton is the best source for information—or the lack thereof. "I really don't know why they are even called demon masks," he continues. "As far as I am aware, none of these beads are mentioned specifically in texts from the period, so most of what we say about their actual meaning to the people who used them is guesswork. In general, though, they are associated with wealthier graves, and were probably a luxury item. As I mention in the Timeline book, demon charms and masks (including Pazuzu, the demon from Washington's own *Exorcist*), were usually protective against some even worse demon." (See the article on the Exorcist Stairs in this book.)

Looking at other highlights, Bead Museum Vice President Hilary Whittaker—who's also the museum's Founding President and the timeline's coordinator—is quick to point out an artifact she herself donated, an amber bead from Africa. "It's been broken," she explains, "and in Africa what they do is repair them with metal, which they ram right into the beads. That metal becomes a decoration and enhances the value of the beads."

The faience fists (or *figa* pendants), it turns out, are Roman amulets, "used as a protective, or apotropaic, amulet, in particular, to ward off the evil eye," Lankton writes. "Of course, in later times, and perhaps earlier as well, the fist with the thumb protruding between the first two fingers has a strong sexual connotation." Whittaker points out another ancient bead that similarly combines protection with sexual imagery. "Often overlooked by the casual observer, there's a grotesque little bead that doubles your luck with both phallic and eye imagery that represents two early Roman apotropaic symbols," she writes in an email follow-up to our interview. "Phallic symbols in the Roman world had more to do with luck than sex, and were put on infants and children to protect them from the evil eye."

Whittaker's also excited about the growing collection of pieces from American glass bead artists, found at the most modern end of the timeline. While European glass artisans stick close to techniques developed in guilds dating back to the sixteenth century, their American counterparts have broken away from tradition in startling ways, Whittaker says. You'll immediately notice that these contemporary beads have the brightest colors and most fanciful shapes of any in the exhibit. Those features are the result of modern technology that allows for higher firing temperatures. In fact, behind the progression of beads across time is the steady advance of techniques for drilling holes, refining metals, and making glass and ceramics. Certain materials or styles show up on the timeline depending on when they were invented.

The timeline's catalog provides fascinating backgrounds for every bead, detailing cultural context, history, materials, and manufacture. The display is completed by wall maps showing the pertinent countries and cultures represented, and a large wall chart taken from Lois Sherr Dubin's gigantic tome, *History of Beads*, which was the inspiration for the museum's exhibit. Seeing a bead timeline printed on paper is one thing, but seeing the beads up close is much more captivating. They're so fascinating, you might wonder why no one else has done this, but on its website the Bead Museum claims to be the first to mount "such an extensive, representative exposition of world beads...with identifying information."

One reason for that uniqueness is simple; putting the Bead Timeline together wasn't easy. The beads are arrayed on cushioned panels, with cleverly deployed strings that separate them into geographic regions. "There are about 5,000 beads, if you can believe it. It doesn't look like it, but let me tell you there are," Whittaker laughs. "'Cause we've mounted every cotton pickin' one of 'em! And it's an unbelievable work. It took seven weeks of two curators working with me at my house. We just worked around the clock."

The timeline was designed to be expanded; the strings can move to accommodate new acquisitions. "And they have been moved several times already," Whittaker reveals. "Which is another unbelievably dastardly work to do." Already, there are numerous beads waiting to be added—so many that Whittaker is currently preparing another cabinet that will expand the timeline from thirty-five to almost forty feet.

Despite the attractiveness of the Bead Timeline's marvels, you may still wonder why these tiny objects deserve their own museum. Whittaker has a pretty good answer. "Since the beginning of man 30,000 years ago, the first instincts are for survival," she begins. "You've got to put a roof over your head, and you've got to put food in your belly. The next thing is to decorate yourself. And that means beads. Because beads are the indigenous things that are everyman's decorative items...Now, through that decoration we proclaim many things. We identify ourselves in terms of our tribes or our ethnology; we identify our likes and our dislikes, our sense of style, and our wealth. Just as in clothing. We decorate ourselves, and that says who we are. In addition, they're used to mark life rituals and passages."

In light of all that, the Bead Museum's goal is "to effectively tell the story of mankind through beads," says Museum Director Tania Said. A one-room exhibit hall, the Bead Museum may seem a little too small to handle such a huge task—until you remember that the objects of its focus are themselves miniscule. If every bead is socially and historically relevant (and the Bead Museum makes a great case for that), then this museum contains enough material to equal a much larger institution.

The museum is divided into four sections: a space for feature shows, the Bead Timeline, a library, and a small gift shop. The largest section is reserved for feature exhibits that focus on the cultural or social value of beads, like the exhibit, "Naga Tribal Adornment," which closed in December

2004. This show explored the use of beads by the Naga people from a province in the far east of India near Myanmar (once known as Burma). Belts, collars, necklaces, and other objects are formed from extensive beadwork, and everything the Naga wear has meaning, expressing social status and tribal identity.

Wooden mannequins dressed in the costume of warriors from the Ao, Chang, and Kongak tribes showed the diversity of their cultures. Each modeled beaded collars and belts in different combinations to create a fearsome appearance and provide protection as they conducted headhunting raids. The most startling manifestations of their principle cultural obsession are their "head-taker bags," shown in the nearby glass cases. These woven baskets are decorated with the skulls of monkeys and hornbills, boars' tusks, and feathers. The monkey skulls in particular represent human heads taken in the raids. Other monkey skulls are worn on necklaces, but the oddest adornment on display may have been the necklace made of three rodent skulls, the eyes filled by cowrie shells.

The women use their beadwork like clothing, tying belts made from thousands of tiny glass seed beads around their waists as a kind of skirt. Thick bead collars worn in groups become a shirt-like covering. Photographs and numerous examples of these beaded objects provided a complete view of the Naga's use of beads. Like the Textile Museum (see article in this book), the Bead Museum details the social significance and aesthetic value of the materials on display.

The Bead Museum was founded in 1995 by the Bead Society of Greater Washington (BSGW), a group of "scholars, collectors, enthusiasts, and people who are interested in beadwork...But the one connector is an interest in the history and culture of beads," Said says. The first exhibition they put together opened in 1996 at the DC Design Center before the museum opened. That initial show, "Luminesence," focused on contemporary glass beads. They subsequently mounted two other small exhibits at the Martin Luther King Library, in DC, before moving into the second floor at 400 Seventh Street in 1997. Here, they created larger semiannual shows, focusing on African beads, amulets of South Asia, glassworks from Czechoslovakia, and the role of beads in the development of trade. In 2001, the museum moved downstairs to its current location on the ground floor. Suddenly visible from the street, attendance dramatically increased for the museum's subsequent exhibit featuring beads from Venice, Italy. Shows on contemporary glass beads (called "The Audacious Bead"), works in silver, and the Naga beads followed in turn.

These major exhibitions allow the museum to tell the story of beads in greater depth, focusing on they way they reveal "who we are, what we are, and what we know at a particular time and place," Said notes. And while the timeline is composed of individual beads, Said points out, the larger shows present beads "composed for either aesthetic or cultural reasons. And the Naga exhibit is a fantastic illustration of how beads are assembled by groups of individuals in a particular society to symbolize something. 'Audacious Beads' was something quite different, because it was really about beads as an aesthetic medium. It was creating artwork using beads. Those beads didn't necessarily have significance on their own individually like what you saw in the Naga exhibition."

Another recent show, "The Universal Bead: How It Unites Us All," opened in January 2005. Something of an attempt to unite the themes of the previous shows, the exhibit explains the worldwide fascination with beads, comparing the ways different cultures across history have used, interpreted, and valued beads to satisfy fundamental human needs. In addition to glass cabinet displays, a documentary film, "World on a String" helps explain the complex cultural interactions at work.

That's a big job for a little object that Said says can be defined as, "Anything with a hole through it. It really is that simple." Then she adds, "Sometimes people get really philosophical and ask if that means rubber bands and smoke rings! It depends if they're strung, possibly."

Smoke ring necklaces? Look for them in the Bead Timeline's future!

Belly Dancing Capital of the USA: DC's Golden Age of the Danse Oriental

Includes Mondo Belly Dance: A Guide to DC Area Restaurants Featuring Belly Dancing

If Salome had come to Washington in the 1960s to perform the dance of the seven veils, she'd have taken second billing to Adriana. Chances are good Salome would have come here only because of Adriana to check out her astonishing back bends and intricate hand work, visit a workshop at her dance school, or just bask in her presence. And Salome would have had to fight through the crowds for a view.

From the moment Adriana arrived from Boston in 1961 to dance at the newly opened Port Said nightclub (at 1418 Eye St.), she meant business—show business, that is. Fueled by her serious talent, the opulence of the Port Said, and crowds of conventioneers, the Middle East dance scene in Washington exploded, becoming the hottest in the country for more than a decade.

It's difficult to picture such a scene, but *Baltimore News-Post* columnist Jimmy Colimore made the attempt several times in the 1960s: "Spectacularly-proportioned Adriana is the featured torso-tosser at the Suez, the colorful Near Eastern nitery on 14th St," he wrote. On another occasion he effused: "The magic of Adrienne [sic] is again holding Acropolis show-goers enchanted. The auburn-haired oriental beauty is hailed as the greatest beauty ever to appear at the Acropolis...She is an emotional experience... expert in the art of flexing and unflexing the abdomen." And in a moment of hipsterized inspiration, Colimore babbled: "Her endless eye-mazing mid-riff movements set blood pressures soaring."

If that doesn't sound like the DC you know, you ain't heard nothing yet. While Californians were sipping mai tais and dancing the hula, Washingtonians were belly dancing. A Port Said show was an exhausting, exhilarating affair, with a live band of the country's best Middle Eastern musicians starting at 8:30 p.m. and continuing without pause until 2 a.m. as seven belly dancers performed two sets a night. In between sets, the dancers played small percussion instruments or swirled with the throngs of restaurant patrons who swarmed the stage. Customers threw copious amounts of cash on the entertainers to show their appreciation, as in the old Greek custom. This tip money, amounting to thousands of dollars, was swept up and split among the musicians and dancers. With some variations over the nights and years, this scene remained the same into the 1970s at the Astor and other clubs.

Already a star dancer in her native Boston in the late 1950s, Adriana first visited the Port Said at the invitation of its owner, George Harris. The quality of the food, the live band, the decor—and the dressing rooms—induced her to make it her new home base. "George Harris was very commercial. What I mean was that he ran his club on an American scale," Adriana says in a still-thick Boston accent. "The place was packed all the time, standing room only. It was a line like a movie theater. By nine o'clock, there was no way to get in." Harden and Weaver frequently talked up Adriana's performances on their popular morning radio show on WMAL. In the 1970s, TV weatherman Willard Scott called her to play his secretary in a televised skit honoring Harden and Weaver's Tenth Anniversary. "I came on and threw my coat off and began to dance," she recalls. "The crowd went wild."

Naturally, political figures were drawn to the scene, too. "I could tell you some stories—senators being thrown out because they were bad boys," Adriana says. She recalls that the night JFK was assassinated, members of his cabinet were expected at the Syriana restaurant, where she also performed. Adriana became the most photographed dancer of her time and often appeared on television.

After the Port Said established the lure of the *danse du ventre*, Harris then opened the Suez. The Syriana on Connecticut and M Streets advertised its Harem Room by declaring: "Pleasure rules there until 4 a.m." Another premier spot, the Astor, at 1813 M St., opened in the 1950s as a restaurant, and owner Bessie Zaras brought in belly dancing in 1961. Later DC clubs included the Black Ulysses, the Algiers on Wisconsin Avenue, the Greek Village, and the Salaam Supper Club. The scene spread to National Press Club and embassy parties—like the one at the Moroccan Embassy covered in a 1966 *Newsweek* article that featured an appearance by Adriana (who rushed over between sets at the Astor). Baltimore's main club, the Acropolis, was supplemented by the Torch Club, the Zorba, and the James House. Suburbs in both Maryland and Virginia also had their clubs.

It wasn't long before Washington was the country's premier spot for Middle Eastern dance, beating out former champ Boston and New York's 8th Avenue hot spots, mostly because Adriana brought many of the better musicians and dancers to town from both cities, and because local clubs were of a higher caliber. The Port Said band soon included inspiring bouzouki player John Tatassopoulos, violinist Freddie Elias, kanoon players Emile Kasses and Emin Gunduz, and oud player Sami Shayed. Many of these musicians appeared on albums and still live in the area. [Tatassopoulos died of cancer in 2000.] Famous "music for belly dancing" recording artist Eddie Kochak regularly came down from New York for gigs, and made Adriana the first American belly dancer to appear on a record sleeve—his 1963 Decca album *Ya Habibi*. Other dancers included Aset, Emar Gamal, Nadina, Ozel Turkbas, Jameela Omar, and Delilah, as well as in later years Fairouz Samar, Adina, Antonia, Athanasia Georganas, and Tahia. The music and dance covered Greek, Egyptian, Persian, Armenian, and Turkish folk styles. As clubs opened and closed over the years, dancers and musicians circulated through them and even toured. Dancers regularly came from other cities to work or check out the action.

But always at the center of the Washington scene was Adriana, who brought a new level of excitement and professionalism to the *danse oriental*. "She brought class to this dance," Fairouz Samar recalls. "She made it entertainment. She instilled pride; she brought respect to the dance." Known as "The Jewel of the Nile" from the time she started in 1968 at the Acropolis, Samar was one of Adriana's star pupils and considered her double in the dance. Samar worked in New York for five years in the early 1970s, where she often heard about Adriana's accomplishments.

As none of the television footage of her survives, it's fortunate for Washington historians that Adriana remembers quite well the qualities that distinguished her dancing. "It was my style on the stage; I had lots of class, lots of spunk, lots of personality," she says matter-of-factly. "I changed history when I came into the picture as a Middle Eastern dancer because of my beautiful turns, my classic style, my hand movements. [I was] very sensual on the stage, very comic on the stage. I knew how to control my audience, because I came from the American field of dance, which was the big supper night clubs. As a jazz dancer I worked all over the world with the big stars, Frank Sinatra, Sammy Davis, Jr, all of them."

As you can expect, Adriana doesn't like the b-word. "The word 'belly dancer' is a slam," she insists. "I don't come from belly dancing, I come from show business. My background in classical ballet, jazz and modern dance made me a better dancer, plus I did a lot of research on the dance."

One of Adriana's earliest and greatest successes as a teacher was Ibrahim Farrah, known as Bobby when he came to the Port Said as a customer after classes at George Washington University. Because of his enthusiasm, Adriana would bring him on stage to dance. Farrah worked as a waiter at Syriana while she served as his mentor. Eventually he moved to New York City and started the Near East Dance Group, a troupe famous worldwide for its authenticity and quality. Farrah later repaid Adriana with an award at one of his company's Kennedy Center performances in 1977.

The Port Said closed its doors in 1969 after the riots that followed Martin Luther King's assassination. Although work was still plentiful at other clubs, such as the Astor and Acropolis, the scene declined in the 1970s. After a mastectomy in 1972, Adriana redesigned her costumes and kept dancing. Later that year, she opened the Mecca of Middle Eastern Dance, located across Wisconsin Avenue from the Algiers, in Georgetown. The first licensed and bonded school of its kind, the Mecca took in 400 students a week at its peak. Adriana offered instruction in many dance styles, as well as in make-up, skin care, costume making, and music theory, and she was the first to offer workshops in Middle Eastern dance.

By 1982, when Adriana closed the Mecca's doors, the "Golden Age" was long over. Adriana herself had weathered numerous personal tragedies, including the deaths of her husband and stepchildren. Starting in 1992, she produced a series of annual comeback shows, the Middle Eastern/ Mediterranean Dance Oriental Gala Revue and Awards Ceremony. More recently, she produced reviews at Alekos Taverna, in Wheaton, Maryland, featuring her students and Golden Age dancer Delilah with the restaurant's house band. The musicians included one of Tatassopoulos's young students on oud. The shows inspired hopes of a revival of the 1960s scene, but they were missing the star attraction. Since her hip replacement, Adriana is leaving the dancing to others.

Mondo Belly Dance: A Guide to DC Area Restaurants Featuring Belly Dancing

Casablanca, 1504 King St., Alexandria, VA. (703) 549-6464. Website: www.moroccanrestaurant.com. Belly dancing takes place every night at 8:00 p.m. On Saturdays, the regular belly dancing show occurs at 7:30 and 8:30 p.m., plus a special "Arabic Nights" show from 10:30 p.m. to 2:00 a.m., that features a live, four-piece Arabic band accompanying the belly dancers. Cover charge for Arabic Nights show is $10. Moroccan cuisine with both prix fixe and a la carte menus. Vegetarian options.

Marrakesh, 617 New York Ave. NW, WDC. (202) 393-9393. Website: www.marrakesh.us. Like attending a royal Moroccan feast, a dinner at Marrakesh is a legendary event. All guests are seated at the same time in a giant room on low couches. There are two seatings nightly, and you must call for reservations. From ritual handwashing (you eat with your fingers!) to the dramatic pouring of mint tea at the meal's end, the service is impeccable. The belly dancer appears in the middle of the room at just the right moment during the courses and shimmies to prerecorded music.

Be sure to check the brag wall of photos on the way to the restrooms, including one vintage 1970s shot of Warren Beatty shimmying with a belly dancer. Moroccan cuisine with prix fixe menu only. Vegetarian option available.

Marrakesh de Paris, 14418 Layhill Rd., Silver Spring, MD. (301) 438-1100. Belly dancers every Friday and Saturday at 8:30 p.m. with prerecorded music. Reservations recommended. Moroccan and Parisian cuisine. Vegetarian options.

Memsahib, 4840 Boiling Brook Pkwy., Rockville, MD. (301) 468-0098. Website: www.memsahibrestaurant.com. Offers six course prix fixe menu of Indian cuisine and belly dancing nightly at 8 p.m. to prerecorded music. Reservations required. Vegetarian options.

Meze, 2437 18th St. NW, WDC. (202) 797-0017. Website: www. mezedc.com. Belly dancing lessons offered Sunday nights at 10 p.m. Come and observe, but you may be drawn into the dance! Music provided by DJ Modern. This hip restaurant in the Adams Morgan neighborhood offers a Turkish and Mediterranean menu. Vegetarian options.

Pars, 10801 Lee Hwy, Fairfax, VA. (703) 273-3508. Website: www. pars-restaurant.com. Belly dancing takes place every Friday at 8 and 9:15 p.m., and on Saturday at 8:15 and 10:30 p.m., with Persian music at 9:30 p.m. Dancers include Nimeera (her candelabra dance is not to be missed), Yasmina, Shahrzad, and Amustela—you can check their schedules and photos on the website! Call for reservations. Offers extensive menu of Persian cuisine. Vegetarian options.

Shalimar, 3263 M St. NW, WDC. (202) 338-5736. Belly dancing on Friday and Saturday from 11:00 p.m. to 3:00 a.m., accompanied by a four-piece live band and two vocalists. Middle Eastern cuisine. Vegetarian options.

Skewers, 1633 P St. NW, WDC. (202) 387-7400. Website: www. skewers-cafeluna.com. Belly dancing on Saturday nights at 9:00 p.m. to prerecorded music. Lebanese cuisine. Vegetarian options.

Tabouleh, Kentland's Square, 644 Center Point Way, Gaithersburg, MD. (301) 963-3773. Belly dancing every Saturday at 10:30 and 11:15 p.m. Lebanese cuisine.

Taste of Morocco, 3211 N. Washington Blvd. (at corner with Wilson Blvd), Arlington, VA. (703) 527-7468. Website: www.tasteofmorocco. com. Belly dancing takes place from Wednesday to Sunday at 8:30 p.m. Reservations recommended. Comfortable restaurant in Clarendon neighborhood has seating at tables and low couches along the walls and an extensive menu of Moroccan cuisine available in prix fixe specials and a la carte. Vegetarian options.

Tel Aviv Cafe, 4867 Cordell Ave., Bethesda, MD. (301) 718-9068. Website: www.americascuisine.com/dc/telavivcafe.html. Belly dancing Saturdays at 9:30 p.m. to prerecorded music. Mediterranean and French cuisine. Vegetarian options.

The Big Chair

2100 block of Martin Luther King, Jr. Avenue, SE
Riverview Plaza
Washington, DC
Hours: Anytime
Cost: Free

For a time, DC was king of the Big Chair wars.

In the 1950s, Bassett Furniture Industries, of Bassett, Virginia, appreciated Curtis Brothers' furniture company so much that they made them something really special to set outside their Nichols Avenue showroom in Washington, DC's Anacostia neighborhood. Because Bassett made chairs and Curtis Brothers sold them, it seemed natural that the monument would take the form of, you guessed it, a chair. But not just any chair. A Duncan Phyfe model chair standing nineteen feet, two and a half inches tall and made of solid African mahogany wood from the Belgian Congo. The chair stands even taller on a four foot high concrete base. A photograph of the July 7, 1959, dedication ceremony shows five people standing on the seat of the chair with plenty of room for more. They were on top of the world, chairwise.

Not only did the "World's Biggest Chair" honor Curtis Brothers' community service, ability to move lots of Bassett product, and long standing as an Anacostia employer, it was also designed to crush Thomasville, North Carolina's claim to having the biggest chair, at a paltry eighteen feet tall. Thomasville's chair was also a Duncan Phyfe model, but it was made of steel and concrete.

Both chairs were quickly outdone by small cities across the U.S. desperate for a claim to fame: Morristown, Tennessee; Gardner, Massachusetts; Binghamton, New York; Lipan, Texas... And the race continues. For the record, Roadside America lists the tallest chair at thirty-three feet, a steel monstrosity residing in Anniston, Alabama. (For more chair mania, visit Roadside America on the web at: www.roadsideamerica. com/set/CIVIchair.html.)

Don't bother asking the Big Chair how it got there—it's not talking. For information on its history, you have to go to the source. John Edwin (Jeb) Bassett III, Vice President of Global Sourcing at Bassett Furniture, has done just that, cracking the company's Big Chair file and graciously reading me highlights from contemporary news accounts over the phone. Jeb Bassett himself wouldn't remember the chair. "The chair was built in

1958, and my father supervised construction of the chair," he says. "I was born the day this chair left Bassett, Virginia, headed for Washington, so my father was late gettin' up there."

Bassett's files clarify a few basic facts. While most web sources credit the chair as a nineteen and one half foot tall construction of mahogany from Honduras, the company's records show it to be a slightly shorter construction of African mahogany. But Jeb knows much more about DC's Big Chair. "The seat is 113 inches wide, and 144 inches deep," he reads, flipping through a couple different sources. "It weighs 4,600 lbs. The chair is fastened together with seven-eighths inch leg bolts. The type of glue used was Cascophen glue made by the Borden Company. And engineers from the Dupont Company put the original finishing material on the chair. It took eleven-hundred man hours to build the chair. To truck the chair to Washington, special permits were obtained from the highway department so that the route could cut out certain low underpasses."

Another company employee, twenty year Bassett veteran Junior Amos, sheds some light on the transport of the Big Chair. A construction manager who helped build and ship Bassett's most recent big chair (a touring model intended for promotional purposes), Amos has the proper background. "[The 1958 model] could be took apart, and that's how they got it up there," Amos says. "It was made in pieces. It comes apart and lays down, the way I understand it. The one I just made doesn't come apart. We moved it on a hydraulic machine that lays it back on the trailer."

So Curtis Brothers must have been a pretty special retailer to deserve such an awesome reward. But how special were they exactly? "They were one of our best customers," Jeb Bassett says. "I don't know if they were *the* best customer." Flipping through some more papers, he thinks he may have found an answer in a story published in the local Henry County, Virginia, paper in 1958. "'Bassett Furniture Industries has completed the construction of the largest chair in the world," Bassett begins reading.

The article continues: "'The chair will be placed on permanent display in the parking lot of a large retail furniture store in Washington, DC. Robert Niver, Advertising Director for Bassett Industries, says the firm is Curtis Brothers. He also says the retail outlet is one of the most promotional-minded he knows of. For instance, all customers are greeted by a charming receptionist, and all clerks wear uniforms with fresh flowers in their lapels. The store has a wishing well in which customers place their wishes each month. One person is awarded whatever she wished for per month. Another interesting thing, Mr. Niver says, is the fact that every delivery is made in a white truck with a captain and a driver. When the new furniture is taken to a home, the captain goes to the front door and salutes the housewife snappily, and then reports he is at her service. And a carpet is taken off the truck and laid inside the house to the room where the new furniture is to be placed. After the furniture is in place, the crew polishes it, sees that all drawers or whatever are working, and then offers to move any other furniture inside the house that the owner wants moved. That sort of service sure has paid off for them.'"

When Bassett Furniture Industries celebrated their centennial in 2002, Jeb recalls, "We wanted the chair back. While [Curtis Brothers] had a fine career, they eventually closed the business, and the chair, I guess, went to their creditors. We were told it had become a regional landmark, and we couldn't have it back. So we built a bigger chair two years ago."

The Bassett Company's new chair stands at twenty feet, three inches. With a mission-style design constructed of ash wood and modeled after their Grove Park collection, the chair follows contemporary tastes. Plus, it makes a great advertisement, so the company sent it on a tour of furniture showrooms across the country. As you can guess, Bassett Furniture is still going strong. (Should you need some chairs and stuff, visit their website at www.bassettfurniture.com.)

Washington's Big Chair has seen a few changes over the years. Curtis Brothers closed in 1973, and the street name has changed from Nichols Avenue to Martin Luther King, Jr. Avenue. But the chair still reigns supreme over all it surveys in Anacostia, even though it's looking a little shabby these days. The tan padded cushion seems to be upholstered in vinyl, hardly the most comfortable seating material, but worse than that, the paint is peeling off, and the legs are rotting near the chair's feet.

If you were willing to risk your life on the decaying structure, you might actually be able to climb up onto the Big Chair and take a seat. From that vantage point, you'd face the large brick office building at 2100 Martin Luther King, Jr. Avenue. Riverview Plaza (formerly the Curtis Brothers' warehouse, and now home to DC Lottery) would be at your back. You probably wouldn't be able to see the Anacostia River over the Anacostia Professional Building on your left (once the Curtis Brothers' showroom and offices), but you'd be master of the commercial strip right around the base of the chair. You'd certainly deserve your fifteen minutes of self-importance. But to truly enjoy the big chair, you may not need to to go vertical.

That's because just standing below it one feels a curious excitement, a sense of majesty or wonder. There's something truly inspiring about an object as useless as a really big chair.

The Black Fashion Museum

2007 Vermont Avenue, NW
Washington, DC 20001
(202) 667-0744
Website: www.members.aol.com/money4bfm/BFM/splash.
html
Hours: By appointment only
Cost: $3

If I feel like I'm being welcomed to Joyce Bailey's home whenever I visit the Black Fashion Museum, it's not just because she's the museum's executive director, or that she owns this small Shaw neighborhood townhouse. She's also the daughter of museum founder Lois Alexander-Lane. I love the way the Black Fashion Museum capitalizes on its smallness. You need an appointment to visit, but that guarantees you a warm welcome and a patient tour guide to identify the displayed items and answer questions. There's no rush. Bailey lingers over everything, letting you find your way and proudly detailing the museum's history.

Although the museum preserves 3,000 garments made by Black designers on the second floor, the small exhibit space displays just a dozen or so items at a time—yet it's crowded with fascinating stories. One past show featured evening wear from the 1920s made by Black dressmakers for the intimate spaces of jazz clubs and dance floors that defined the feeling of energy, movement, and freedom of the time. Two costumes designed by Geoffrey Holder for the Broadway version of *The Wiz* highlighted the whimsical side of another show, "Lights, Cameras, Costumes: Designers for the Stars." The Tin Man costume combines replicas of galvanized tin trashcans, license plates, and other scraps to capture a street-level junkyard aesthetic, while "Addaperle, the Good Witch of the North" was represented by her blue and white patchwork dress with appliquéd magician's gloves.

The collection includes celebrities' clothes, too, like the fringed white dresses once worn by the New Supremes in the 1970s. These were "given to my mother by Stephen Burrows, who designed them," Bailey says. There's a dress once worn by singer and actress Diahann Carroll, a suit from Ben Vereen—and a cream silk dress with sequins and beaded bird details, designed by Zelda Wynn. Just some old thing That Bad Eartha worked on a late-1950s concert stage. "My mother met Ms. Kitt on a couple occasions," Bailey remembers, "and that [sequined gown] was given to her for the museum by Ms. Kitt."

And, of course, the museum owns a typically wild costume from Michael Jackson, dating to his days with the Jackson 5. "It's a novelty African print," Bailey says, remaining calm as the description goes further over-the-top, "with a butterfly top that has a picture of the Jacksons, and a pair of denim hot pants. They were donated in 1974." Hopefully, all these celebrity garments will make it into a future show. There are 5,000 pieces total, Bailey notes; "That's not just costumes, it's also memorabilia and other artifacts."

One of the most striking pieces displayed in the past few years is a simple silk print dress made by Rosa Parks. While Parks' courage during her famous bus ride was changing the course of American history, this dress rested in a shopping bag at her feet. Although draped rather awkwardly on a dressmaker's mannequin, this empty piece of clothing spoke eloquently about personal aspirations, social class, and the strength of dignity. If such storytelling is the intended role of any costume—and the ultimate ambition of any designer—then this garment is second to none.

The Black Fashion Museum started with a challenge that founder Lois Alexander-Lane could not refuse. As a graduate student at the Harlem Institute of Fashion, she was told by a professor that Blacks had made no significant contributions to fashion design. Believing this to be untrue, Alexander-Lane uncovered a vast history of Black contributions to American fashion. Her master's thesis, *The Role of the Negro in Retailing in New York City from 1863 to the Present*, laid the foundation for the first Black Fashion Museum in Harlem, which opened in 1979. A DC native, Alexander-Lane opened a branch here in 1988 as a mobile museum, and in 1993, the whole collection was moved to its current location at 2007 Vermont Avenue, NW.

The townhouse itself has a fascinating back story. Built in 1887 as a private home, it was used as a meeting place for the Ladies Mutual Relief, a Black organization started to raise funds for health care and burials for poor families. At the turn of the nineteenth century, the building housed another charitable organization, the Sojourner Truth Home for Women and Girls, that helped women find work and hosted social visits. There is also evidence that the house was a stop on the Underground Railroad. Alexander-Lane bought the property in 1950, opening the Needle Nook, a boutique "specializing in custom designs and dressmaking." She closed the business when her government job moved her to New York, and she later returned to DC with her museum.

One of Alexander-Lane's triumphs was to correctly identify the designer of Jacqueline Bouvier's wedding dress. The future Mrs. John F. Kennedy sought out only one dressmaker, a descendent of slaves who worked exclusively for members of the social register, and told her: "I want a tremendous dress, a typical Ann Lowe dress." That Ann Lowe dress has been seen and remembered by millions—but the identity and race of the designer was hidden for decades until confirmed by the Black Fashion Museum. The museum documents this achievement only with a photograph, but it does own other samples of Lowe's work.

Inspired by the property's link to nineteenth century Black activist Sojourner Truth, the 2004 show, "Truth: The Fiber of Our Lives," illuminated her life with pertinent objects from the collection. Born an illiterate slave who spoke only the Dutch language of her masters, Isabelle Baumfree gradually freed her mind and then escaped slavery, renaming herself to express her calling as a pilgrim dedicated to liberation for Blacks, women, and the poor. Visualizing Truth's challenges is made easier by the presentation of two slave dresses—one long enough to fit the activist's six-foot frame—as well as a nineteenth century quilt featuring patterns used by the Underground Railroad, and a mangled slave's boot found in the ceiling of a DC home known to be a stop on the "Liberty Line." The simple dignity of these few objects—and the power of the stories they represent—send chills down the spine.

The Black Fashion Museum turned twenty-five on October 21, 2004, but most of the celebration will occur in 2005, when their traveling exhibition, "A Stitch in Time, 1800-2000," returns home. "Because the space we have here is limited, we're breaking it up into three sections," Bailey says. "1800s to the 1920s would be the first section, then going from the 1930s to the 50s, and then the 60s to the present. These would be actual costumes from the period, and all designed by Black designers." That last section is sure to include the return of Rosa Parks' dress to the display rooms.

If the Black Fashion Museum looks from the outside like it could use some dressing up, its contents are as astonishing as those of museums with much greater glamour. Washington may not be known for its fashion sense—or its fashion designers—but as the first museum of its kind, the Black Fashion Museum is one place in town that's making fashion history.

Bull Run Castle

24600 James Monroe Highway
Aldie, VA
(703) 327-4113
Hours: 8 a.m.-8 p.m. daily, except Sun 1-8 p.m.
Cost: $2.50

The massive structure rises more than fifty feet out of the cornfields along Route 15, stuck here between a new town home development in Prince William County and Gilbert's Corner in Loudoun County, Virginia. You can't miss this giant rectangle with round towers on each corner, a gorgeous central panel of brick, and a strangely notched top edge that looks like square teeth on the bottom half of a jaw. As you pass, you might remember that these "teeth" are called crenulations, and that you usually only see them in pamphlets for British vacations. Come to think of it, the whole scene seems to be transplanted from Scotland, with a jagged blue line of mountains in the distance and that castle—a castle!—set just off the highway.

That can't be right. So you pull into the gravel drive, rumbling through the gate to stop before the six foot tall prefabricated cement gargoyle that guards the turn in front of the building. You read the sign: Bull Run Castle. The words make it more real, sort of. But not more real than close proximity to the structure itself. No mirage was ever so massive. Further around the circle, a sign reads, "This is not a museum"—so don't ask. Next to it, another sign advertises "fine antiques," and now you have your reason to park the car. You're not being nosy—you're browsing!

You're likely to see the man who made the castle before you talk to him. He's a rough-looking, sturdy old fellow, with a head of thick white hair, wearing dirt-stained khaki shorts belted at the waist, and an ancient white t-shirt. You might easily confuse him with the hired help and ask, "Who built this place?"

"I did," the old man replies.

OK, but what about the brickwork, the electricity, the plumbing, the fancy front door?

"Read my lips," he says firmly. "I built the castle. Electric, plumbing, heat, carpentry, masonry, marble, tile, flooring, roofing, digging, concrete footers, chimneys, walls, ceilings. Sure I built the castle, yes, everything."

Now you're going to ask the question everybody does, but don't hold back. The man expects it, relishes it. In fact, he offers a tour at $2.50 a head just so he can ask the question—and answer it—himself. "Big question: Why did this dummy here build a castle?" He doesn't wait for you to nod, but rushes ahead with his reasons. "I wanted an antique shop all my life; never wanted to pay rent. Detest the idea of more than about a two minute commute. Figured if I built a castle I'd attract people farther out. That's the real reason, but completely inadequate for any sane person to start a job of this size with so little money," he says in one breath. "I knew I could do it, and knew it would take a long time. To lock myself in, back in 1980 I told all my friends: 'I'm going to build a castle.' Then I had to."

You've just met John Roswell Miller and learned just about everything you need to know about him. The next hour in his company, as he squires you through his life's work, will only confirm all the unspoken facts of his first statement: that he has a stubborn streak a mile wide, an infinite capacity for hard labor, and an ego bigger than either of these other traits. Nevermind that he's surrounded by Civil War battlegrounds, rampaging exurban sprawl, millionaire horse enthusiasts, celebrity residents like Robert Duvall, and the foothills of the Shenandoah Mountains, Miller has single-handedly erected his own monument, built his own history, and carved his own myth in stone, concrete block, and brick.

Miller says he would like to write a book and call it "How to Build a Castle on Sixteen Grand a Year." He knows just how it would begin: "When we came here in 1980, this was a cornfield and a woods, nothing else...From 1980 until '86 we worked on peripheral work. In '86 I sold my home and started the castle. The ten years prior to '86, I averaged $16,000 a year; my wife never worked; I'm not retired from anything; certainly never won the lottery because I never bought a ticket, or ever will—and we built a castle." Miller took the name for his property from the stream and the mountain that previously loaned it out to a nearby Civil War battlefield. The north fork of Bull Run is just a creek where it runs through Miller's land, but the mighty Bull Run Mountain to the west provides a view fit for a king.

His tour patter flows out in an astonishing gush of action verbs that details the hundreds of backbreaking jobs involved in a project this unthinkably huge. "The peripheral work is extensive," Miller says after a brief pause. That's clearly an understatement, but he's only getting started talking about his preparations for building the castle. "Everything you see here we did. It was a cornfield," he continues. "Planted hundreds of trees. Built a barn, barn shed, brick dog house, round masonry well house, and at the bottom next to the crick, we cleared and grubbed everything by hand—it

48

looks like a park. Volleyball court, treehouse, a couple footbridges. Cleared and grubbed a trail by hand twelve foot wide all around the perimeter of our thirteen and a half acres for fire and horses. Built a big pond, a deck over the pond, and gave three acres to my daughter Mary and her family. We built most of her home, too."

Miller and his family had their work cut out for them. From 1980 until 1986, they worked the land only on weekends, driving forty-six miles up from their Ft. Belvoir home on Friday night. They worked all day Saturday and on Sunday afternoon. Sunday morning they went to church; that evening, they drove back home. As they cleared the land, cut a road, and made basic amenities, like a brick outhouse with a conical roof, they lived in a tent. It took them six years to get so sick of commuting and "putting the tent away wet" that they sold their house and moved to the castle grounds permanently. By that time, they had built a little round stone house, with a kitchen and electricity, plus "a wood stove for heat, ladder, trap door, a couple of mattresses, dormer out the back in case of fire," Miller recites. "It was like livin' downtown after the tent."

After a few more years they built a cabin, then they expanded it. Finally, they moved into the castle, which had been going up, block by block, wall by wall, tower by tower. After twenty-odd years, the place is nearly complete, aside from redecorating one room and finishing an escape tunnel. Overlooking these absent conveniences, what does it have? Miller fires off his inventory like he's giving orders: "There's six bedrooms, five full bath, two powder rooms, fourteen closets, eighty-one doors, eighty-nine windows, and a whole lot more. It includes a dungeon, a portcullis, an armory, and firing points all around the periphery."

Such a listing is impressive, but it hardly does justice to the place. Once through the formidable front doors, Miller points to a wooden trapdoor set in the floor that leads to the dungeon. "The dungeon is pretty neat," he croaks. "Two bunks, straw mattress, a table, lantern, a bucket, and two rotten lawyers." Avoiding that pitfall, you move to the barbican, where you can primp before meeting the lord of the manor, should you be visiting more formally. A large stairway divides the grand entrance: to the left, a huge dining room, to the right, the kitchen. Off the dining area there's an ecumenical chapel (Miller has made arrangements for it to be consecrated by his Baptist minister and a rabbi), plus "a wet bar for the Episcopalians."

Upstairs, all the bedrooms are themed. There's the English Tack Room, decorated with hunting motifs in honor of the Virginia Hunt Country, but otherwise still under construction; the "Queen Anne Room"; "La Francais Chambre Coucher," or in the native tongue, "The French Bedroom"; and a Victorian Room. A children's nursery lies in the core of the keep. On the third floor, there's "La Tour a L'Amour" (the "Tower of Love," of course), its walls decorated in shades of pink and copiously sprinkled with cupids and cherubs. It also has a fancy ceiling that features wooden strips branching off from a light fixture like rays of brown sunlight. A giant skylight fills the central stairway with light and heat, and Miller describes how a fan blows this heated air down into the foyer during the winter.

From the barbican to the core of the keep, the place is packed with antiques: furniture, weapons, books, paintings, knickknacks, you name it. "Virtually everything in the castle is for sale," Miller announces. He brags about his low prices, and if you look at something too long, he'll give you a hard sell. It is a working antiques shop, after all, and his main source of income. In the past, he's operated the place as a bed and breakfast inn, but mostly friends and family occupied his fancy guest rooms. He's had better luck renting the place to large groups for special events. The castle is particularly popular with a group of 25 to 75 vampires who have met there sixteen times.

"[The vampires] have a dentist in the area that makes caps for their teeth," Miller says, gesturing to his mouth with two fingers, making pointed fangs. "They play a game something like Dungeons and Dragons. That's pretty neat." You might be astonished that a liberal-baiting old Army man like Miller could tolerate such oddballs, but he seems to genuinely enjoy their visits. A photo of the group hangs in his kitchen, and as he points it out, he recalls, "They don't come until late after sundown and they leave before sunrise. I always have garlic around my neck."

Don't think a lush interior means the exterior is just a fancy cinderblock shell surrounding a suburbanite's McMansion. The castle is built to last—and it's built to be defended. "I know damn well I'm not going to be attacked," he asserts, "but I'll tell you, if John Miller says he's gonna build a castle, you can bet your ass it's gonna work. If I build a merry-go-round, you can get on the damn horse and go around it. If it be a bicycle, you could pedal it."

The brick and block walls are twelve inches thick and over fifty feet tall, set with firing ports so all exterior walls can be seen and defended from the inside. "That way, if it's raining and somebody's screwing around with my walls, I can fire on them and not get wet," Miller notes with considerable satisfaction. The front doors are four and three quarters of an inch thick solid wood, banded in iron.

But those are merely the outer defenses. Should his castle be overrun by invaders—"which I'm certain won't happen," Miller repeats in an attempt to defend himself in advance from charges of paranoia— "I would withdraw into the keep of the castle. The keep is twenty-two foot diameter, four stories high, no windows in the first floor. The second floor is an armory; it just has slit windows around the periphery. Plus two windows to fire down my own hallway. Once you have barricaded yourself inside the keep, in order to have mobility throughout the four floors, I built a center section. I call it the 'core of the keep.' It's approximately four foot diameter. At each level there's an access door, a straight set of stairs, a trap door up, a trap door down, and a firing port." His armory, he adds, is stocked with thirty identical rifles, so that each defender can draw from the same sizable stockpile of ammo.

On the building of the keep, Miller is more than willing to admit to Divine Intervention. His original plan was to use stone dragged from his creek bed (the source of the rock in his walls). Then he stumbled on a company that made concrete blocks; they were going out of business and needed to unload some dead weight, literally. It seems that modern manholes are made from cast concrete, but back in the day, they were assembled from huge curved blocks—blocks just perfect for building a castle keep, should anyone be trying such a thing. Score one for Miller. He picked up 4,700 blocks, "half fifty-five pound, half forty-two pound" for $250 total. "Thank God I found them, because it made it a lot easier," Miller says. "That was a big blessing."

Don't even think of infiltrating Miller's side entrance, either. He spared no pains on this one. "It's barricaded initially with a heavy iron gate, then a door with a drop bar," he says with relish. "Halfway up the stairs is a portcullis, a vertical iron and oak gate that's completely iron bound on the side away from the stairs. That goes down in two seconds."

But the most deadly serious fortification is actually underfoot—it's the ceiling to the cellar, a thick slab of concrete reinforced with steel rods. "It's built so it could take the collapse of the castle on top of it without losing its integrity," Miller says calmly, explaining that a mere eight miles away lies Dulles Airport, a major target for nuclear attack. In these days of airborne terrorists, his security preparations are making more and more sense.

Miller's pride in his accomplishments is tempered only by the frequency with which he has recounted his own legend. He's describing solo labors equal to Hercules but in a deadpan recitation that makes it clear he expected nothing less from himself. To John Miller, these are matters of fact. There's no need to gild the lily. "Nothing's phony about this place, not even me," he says, running backwards down the main stairs while staring me in the eye.

To put it plainly, the amount of detail work in the castle is astonishing. As a carpenter, Miller is proud of the elaborate trim in the "Chambre Coucher Francais." As a mason, he lovingly describes the painstaking effort to chisel a stone-like finish into the concrete slabs that form his kitchen fireplace. As an interior designer, he makes sure I pay special attention to the color scheme of "La Tour Amour": burgundy, pink, and white. "No female had anything to do with decorating this place," Miller grunts from up the stairs. "Most people think men can't do colors." As an architect, he scorns modern practitioners who equate novelty with quality. He prefers the classics, "used since the time of Christ," such as heavy beams, arches, and round rooms. "Sixteen round rooms in the castle! That's a lot," he notes. "Any dummy can make a square or rectangular—or it looks like a square, anyway." That last bit's a jab at corner-cutting framers and drywall men who might fudge a measurement or three. And as an engineer, he crows about the thirty foot arched bridge he built over the creek, boasting that during the construction of his daughter's house they drove a 60,000 pound well truck across it. "I figured any dummy can build a straight bridge; that's pretty easy," he drawls. "I arched mine."

One gets the idea that Miller undertakes these extra jobs out of a sheer love for a challenge that borders on perversity. But in the category of mind-numbing repetition in a task sure to go unrecognized, nothing matches the endless labors of his homemade gravel roads. "They represent probably a hundred loads of free debris brought in and dumped by the state when they were working on the roads," Miller recounts. "They didn't even spread dump; they just dumped. And we took the hunks of asphalt and laid them out like a jigsaw puzzle: fill in, build up, fill in, build up. Then I got thirty loads of crusher run stone, spread dump that carefully, and over a period of over two years I take my '69 Chevy pick up—one of my best friends—get a couple of ton at a time of screenings, the small stones, shoveled it off, built a big drag, and over a two year period pulled that drag around here hundreds of times." Talk about a shocking testimony for sheer perseverance!

Indeed, Miller can't seem to imagine himself without a day's labor in front of him. The castle's completion seems to lie on some imaginary horizon line that will never be reached—not if he can help it. "The castle probably never will be completely finished," Miller asserts. "I have one bedroom I need to get a carpet in and a couple things. Other than that and finishing the tunnel, that's about it."

But don't confuse incompleteness with imperfection. Miller is certain he's done it right. "What's important is that if I were to start the castle tomorrow, knowing precisely what I know today, the castle would be exactly as it is now," he says. "No door swings would change, nothing would change. The only change I would make in the castle if I were starting now, if I had more money, it would be larger. Other than that, I did all the proper prior planning to prevent piss poor performance. I made all the compromises before I started."

John Roswell Miller grew up in Redding, Pennsylvania, and at age eighteen, two days after graduating high school, he became a laborer. He moved up to carpenter's helper and got in a few years as a carpenter before being drafted for the Korean War. While serving in the Army Corps of Engineers for thirteen and a half years, he built rocket bases in Europe, and a railroad in France "from scratch." One major project was building the Churchill Rocket Research Range in Manitoba, Canada, just outside the little town of Churchill known as the "Polar Bear Capital of the World." "We had a wrestling program up there," he remembers, "and I was 'Killer Miller.'" While in the arctic, he met his first wife, a baroness who introduced him to numerous castles in England.

"Very quickly I found that I could cope," Miller says of his military service. "Because I knew how to work. I went to Officer's Candidate School. I got out, no question about my coping, 'cause those ROTC people, a lot of those people couldn't blow their nose. I outshone them. My few years as a carpenter gave me much more insight and skill and know how to build anything. In construction, everything is relative. If you can build something with wood, you can get a good idea how to do it with stone, or steel, or whatever."

Leaving the army in the rank of Major, Miller started his own construction company. He built five custom houses in Mount Vernon and Yacht Haven, Virginia, before he realized he wasn't going to make a profit—or as he succinctly puts it: "Built 'em too good, lost it all." Then from 1964 to 1986, he switched to home additions and decks. By that final year, he was on to the biggest project of his life: building a castle with his bare hands. Solo. With just a little help from his son, two daughters, and a hired man. A few years ago, he separated from his second wife, the mother of his children. "It's amazing how good you can get along with a woman when she moves 160 miles away," he says drily.

By his own admission, Miller is a daredevil, a glutton for physical challenges of any type. "None of my friends will play follow the leader with me," he laments, clearly disappointed with their lack of gumption. But who can blame them? Even if they could forget that Miller's the man who built a castle just to prove he could do it, they've almost certainly seen the old photographs hanging in the back room—the ones of him doing a handstand on top of a seventy-five foot sway pole, diving into a tiny tank of water, walking on broken glass, and lying on a bed of nails. The latter two stunts he performed as part of a fundraising show for the Mount Vernon Woods Citizen's Association. Since he couldn't dance or sing, he came out hawking "Miller's Magic Miracle Medicine"—actually little bottles of whiskey—that he claimed could make one impervious to pain.

The tank dive earned him some pretty good money when he did it in the 1950s. "I bet somebody twenty-five bucks that I could dive twenty foot into thirty inches of water that had a concrete bottom," Miller remembers. "I just figured if I landed right I wouldn't hurt myself at all. I turned my feet out, I turned my head out, and I was absolutely flat. I hit the bottom—of course I hit the bottom. Everything hit the bottom. My arms, everything. I didn't hurt myself because I spread it out. Same reason you can walk on glass. You step on a whole lot of pieces at the same time. The same way you lay on a bed of nails. As long as you're laying on fifty nails, how bad do you get hurt?"

His story of the pole stand is an epic that starts with an innocent Sunday drive with his girlfriend in 1968. They stopped at a little carnival, watching Hungarian aerialist Igor Sandor run through an act involving acrobatic stunts on a high, flexible pole. Miller told his girl, "I can do everything that guy did." She laughed at him. "Which you shouldn't do," Miller advises. He immediately asked Sandor for a shot at the pole, but was turned away. They were taking it down, Sandor explained, but if Miller met the carnival in Woodbridge, Virginia, with a signed affidavit absolving the carnival of all liability, he could take a shot at it. Sandor figured this guy was just trying to impress his girlfriend—that is, until Miller showed up in Woodbridge with the paperwork. The carnies made him wait as Sandor went through his act twice, but when Miller didn't go away, they let him try it. Having memorized the aerialist's routine, Miller climbed up and duplicated the whole act, flawlessly hitting every mark and nailing the grand finale.

"They had these little studs coming out to climb up on, and the last fifteen feet is about an inch and an eighth German steel that really flexes," Miller recalls. Up near the top, he found a crossbar with rings on each end. "You put your arms through there, and it's about that loose," he says, indicating the generous space allowed for his arms. "I got hold of that, threw my feet in the air, and got that son-of-a-gun swinging back and forth, this way, and let it stop, then this way." He marks a cross in the air to show the pattern of his movement. "Went down, and when I got down, they offered me a job."

Miller's completely inadequate reasons for building a castle seem, well, inadequate. One immediately begins groping for other ways to explain his motivations. There are a few potential answers. First of them being that he wanted to test his skills, after a lifetime as a military man and construction worker. Ego gratification is certainly another factor. Miller himself admits—brags even: "My ego has a voracious appetite." Armchair psychologists may have a field day juggling ten-dollar words to describe the condition of an ego that drives a man to build a castle, an empire, or a corporation. But there could be a simpler reason—the most basic reason any man has for doing something monumental. It's the same force that inspired the Taj Mahal and the Trojan Wars. Like these other builders and doers, John Miller has a lost love—a childhood sweetheart who got away fifty-one years ago.

Despite the heavy veneer of military toughness and do-or-die daresmanship, Miller is a softy at heart, a romantic. At the end of my tour, he launches into a long story of his recent reunion with his old flame. After half a century of separation, Miller finally tracked her to a condo outside their hometown, and they've become an item. When he first went to visit her, he says, "As a military man, I'm always armed and ready. I had a box of chocolates in one arm and flowers in the other." In typically overblown Miller style, he made her an elaborate valentine card and birthday gift.

He reveals that on a recent visit he felt dizzy. Went to his doctor—blood pressure up, pulse up from 62 to 76. "I've seen this before," the doctor tells him, "you're in love with that lady you've been telling me about." Miller told his sweetheart it was a sign of his true feelings, because "there isn't a switch on my heart to make it work harder."

Love has had a transformative effect on Miller. He's a lot nicer than I remember him from nearly a decade ago, for one thing. He quit chewing tobacco, and he grew out his hair—he now sports a full white mane with a big cowlick, instead of the severe military buzz cut he favored for decades. And where he used to buy his clothes at Goodwill Industries, Salvation Army, and Walmart, it's Hechts and London Fog for him now.

I can't resist teasing Miller with a little armchair psychoanalysis of my own: Could building the castle be a way of compensating for that lost love?

Feet firmly planted on the ground, Miller offers perhaps the best reason yet to build a castle. "Oh, no. It was just a unique idea to face the future with more than Social Security," he says matter-of-factly. "That's what it was. A very practical solution. As it turns out, everyone used to laugh, but I was right. When I sell, I'll be able to afford to live the way I like to live."

Nothing speaks more highly of Miller's love for this woman than the fact that he's planning to abandon his life's work for her. Once the property sells—for a cool $1.5 million, he hopes—he'll move back to their hometown to live near her. He hopes they'll eventually marry.

Such a move would seem to strike at the core of his being. Will he miss the castle?

"Hell no!" Miller blurts. "It's brick and wood...and you miss people."

And just how will such a subdued, domestic life suit a man accustomed to mighty feats of machismo? "Well, I'm gonna volunteer at the museum," Miller says slowly. "I'm gonna start collecting again; I'm gonna go for coins again. I sold most of my good collections. I'm gonna do a lot of traveling. The first thing we're gonna do is go for a ten day trip on the Mississippi in a steamboat, after I sell the castle."

By the time you get there, John Miller may be off enjoying some well-deserved R & R, but the Bull Run Castle is forever. He made sure of that. Stop by and see it sometime.

Bunny Man Bridge

Colchester Road
Clifton, VA
Hours: Always open
Cost: Free

Stand under the one lane bridge on Colchester Road in Clifton, Virginia, and whisper, "Bunny Man, Bunny Man, Bunny Man." Then prepare yourself. You just called the ghost of a psychokiller who dresses as a white rabbit with big floppy ears. His weapon of choice: an ax. His preferred victim: teenage children.

There are many versions of the Bunny Man story. They commonly involve an escaped lunatic, several murders, and annual hauntings of teenagers drinking under the bridge on Halloween. The classic contemporary account starts the tale in 1903, when a busload of mental patients from a local asylum crashes on the way to Lorton prison. All but two escapees are recaptured: Marcus A. Wallster and Douglas J. Grifon. The men live in the woods, leaving half eaten rabbits as evidence of their existence. Wallster finally turns up dead, his body marked by deep wounds made by a hatchet. Grifon remains at large, eating rabbits, leaving their carcasses in the woods for others to find, and avoiding capture.

The story continues. On Halloween, 1905, a mysterious assailant murders three teenagers at the bridge. The next day, the children are found hanging from the bridge, their throats and chests slashed as if by a small ax. Similar murders occur in 1906, 1913, 1943, 1976, and 1987. Each time, gangs of teenagers are partying under the bridge on Halloween, daring the Bunny Man to return. A light moves down the railroad tracks that cross over the bridge, stopping just over the tunnel. A huge flash of light inside the tunnel signals the beginning of the carnage. Anyone who has dared to stay until midnight is slashed and then hung from the bridge. The few survivors, those who witnessed the incident from a short distance, go insane.

It's fascinating how closely this legend adheres to the standards of modern slasher films, with a supernatural fiend who thirsts for teenage blood and apparently abhors the thought of a few kids getting together for a good time. The ritual nature of the slayings (same time, same murder techniques, same location), as well as their senselessness makes a repeat seem inevitable. A sequel is in the works. Bunny Man 2005, anyone?

But the Bunny Man story didn't always go this way. When tales involving a man dressed in a rabbit suit first started circulating in Fairfax County back in 1970, the maniac was much more benign. He limited his crimes to vandalizing construction sites and menacing young lovers parked on secluded country lanes. The bunny costume was just plain weird, and the hatchet he threw usually missed its target. By the 1980s, the Bunny Man was said to be active in Maryland and DC as well. Around the bridge, his crimes had intensified; the new stories claimed he had murdered 1 to 3 victims, usually children. By the 1990s, the Bunny Man was a supernatural entity striving for ever higher kill counts. He was a psychopath, a serial killer, an urban myth. And he was way too bad to be true.

A Clifton native, Brian Conley became obsessed by the Bunny Man legend in 1976, the year he first heard the story. And when Conley became an Historian-Archivist with the Fairfax County Public Library's Virginia Room, in the City of Fairfax, he had the resources—not to mention the skills—to track the Bunny Man to his roots. Conley started with the 1990s version, quickly discovering that most of the key "facts" had no basis in reality. First, there was never an insane asylum in Fairfax County, Virginia. Second, Lorton Prison wasn't built until 1910, and even then was a DC facility, meaning no Virginia inmates would ever be sent there. Finally, Grifon and Wallster never appear in Fairfax court records.

Conley did dig up a trio of intriguing murders in Fairfax that eerily suggest the 1980s version of the Bunny Man story, although without the rabbit suit. But his big break came when he discovered the Maryland Folklore Archive, part of the University of Maryland's library holdings, and a 1973 term paper called "The Bunny Man." The paper recorded accounts given by Maryland teenagers about the Bunny Man attacks in Fairfax. The kids had heard about them on the television news. Conley dug up the story in the *Washington Post* archives from 1970.

The truth was weirder than he had imagined. There really was a Bunny Man, and he really did attack people and buildings with an ax. Each time, the man in the rabbit costume warned his victims that they were "trespassing." But he didn't hurt anyone, and after two incidents, his activity stopped. Sadly enough for future generations of truth seekers, the Bunny Man was never identified.

In a thorough account of the legend and his investigation entitled "The Bunny Man Unmasked" (available on the web at www.co.fairfax. va.us/library/branches/vr/bunny/bunny.htm), Conley ultimately makes the case that the Bunny Man was an early activist against the urban sprawl that was beginning to claim greater portions of Fairfax County. You see, after World War II, Fairfax was a largely rural county, but by the 1970s, the growing population was fueling a tremendous building boom. Lots of people didn't like seeing cornfields and forests turned into tract housing, although most of them didn't resort to rabbit costumes and scare tactics to fight off development.

Today, people in the neighborhood celebrate the evil legacy of the bridge every Halloween, and teenagers continue to meet there and recount a legend that's over thirty years old. Over the years, the Bunny Man has been spotted in Maryland and DC, and as far south in Virginia as Culpeper. The legend still makes the papers, and even appeared on the Fox Family Channel's *Scariest Places on Earth* program.

Paranormal researchers also flock to the place, looking for evidence of spirit possession. In July 2001, a team from the Baltimore-based Maryland Project arrived and enacted the Bunny Man "summoning ritual," chanting his name three times. Although they heard some strange noises, their photographs showed no unusual lights or auras. The sensitives of the group, however, were convinced there was a faint presence. One heard a girl's voice, and the other detected "the faint sound of a woman screaming." The investigators departed without conclusive evidence, but noted, "We believe this location does have a lot of negative energy associated with it. The possibility that this bridge is haunted is a large one." Read their full report on the web at www.groups.msn.com/MarylandtheoldSupernaturalS tompingGround/themarylandproject.msnw.

The Bunny Man Bridge doesn't have any "official" name, as far as historian Conley knows, but he is certain of a few genuine facts about it. First, the structure technically isn't a bridge at all but a culvert. Second, it was built "about 1910 or 1911, when they punched a second [railroad] track through there." And finally, that the Bunny Man story is just a "great piece of fiction."

"The biggest thing I would press about that bridge is there's nothing to see and no reason to go out there," Conley says indignantly. "The reason I wrote [my article] the way I did, with 6,000 footnotes—which is more than anyone would read—because I hoped someone would refute me. But no one has bothered! I really hoped I'd put a nail in [the Bunny Man's] coffin, but that hasn't done it."

What the heck. How often do you get to see the site of an urban myth? Starting from Chain Bridge Road/Rte. 123 South in Fairfax, Virginia, it's a long drive down Chapel Road to the town of Clifton. You'll pass a Colchester Road on your right—this gravel drive meanders through a buccolic neighborhood and dead ends at a dirt path. At one time, this stretch of Colchester may have connected with the main road that leads to the Bunny Man's legendary haunting ground, but it's not the one you want.

To visit the bridge, you have to continue down Chapel Road several miles until you hit a country town so small the street signs point out the Post Office and the Fire Department. You're in Clifton. Take a right on Main Street, following it across the railroad tracks until it becomes Newman Road. Take a right on Fairfax Station Road, and another right to Colchester, continuing less than a mile until you reach the bridge. Along the way, the large houses are set far back from the road on huge wooded lots, a little bit of country in the Washington, DC, suburbs. From the bridge, no houses are visible. You could stop here virtually undisturbed for hours.

Shaded by trees and overgrowth, the Bunny Man Bridge is more picturesque than spooky. The rural surroundings are calm and quiet, marked only by the pleasant gurgling of a nearby creek, and the distant sounds of dogs barking, cars howling, and planes cruising overhead. There's a crumpled condom on the road, and a few beer cans up near the railroad tracks that pass over the bridge.

Inside the tunnel, someone has scratched "Bunny Man's Watching" into the whitewash. Every sound reverberates, providing the nifty echo effect often used by sound designers to suggest isolation and paranoia. At night, the tunnel must be very dark, as in pitch black. Clifton would make a great setting for "The Legend of Sleepy Hollow," with Ichabod Crane running in terror down Colchester Road into the Bunny Man tunnel to meet his fate.

Even if the Bunny Man is just an urban legend, his story builds personality around a local landmark that otherwise seems rather boring. The fact that the story has stuck, and even continued to grow, speaks to people's need to feel ownership in the history of their communities. In that sense, at least, the Bunny Man has proven to be a good neighbor.

Capital Hauntings Tour

Meets at McPherson Square Metro Station
(White House exit) corner of Vermont & I Streets, NW
Washington, DC
(202) 484-1565
Website: www.washingtonwalks.com
Hours: Wed 7:30 p.m. (April-October); no reservations
necessary
Cost: Adults: $10; children 12 and under: $5

Former First Lady Dolley Madison once ruled Lafayette Square Park. At the turn of the nineteenth century, she was known as Washington's most radiant hostess, as she fulfilled social duties for both Thomas Jefferson (the first bachelor in the White House) and her own husband's administration. After James Madison's death, she carried on at their home, now numbered 1520 H Street, just a block from the presidential mansion. Dolley was so fond of the place that she refused to leave even after she herself passed away. By the mid-1900s, gentlemen leaving the Washington Club just down the street got so used to seeing her ghost sitting on her front porch that they adopted the habit of tipping their hats in her direction, whether the phantom was there or not. Or so the story goes.

There are plenty of other ghost stories set in Lafayette Square, giving Dolley Madison plenty of, um, spirited company. In fact, there are so many ghosts here, tour guide Renee Calarco says, "The area around Lafayette Square Park is thought to be the most haunted spot in all of Washington, DC." And so she begins another Capital Hauntings tour, a nifty way of drawing jaded visitors into the real history of the federal city's earliest years.

Lafayette Square Park lies just north of the White House across Pennsylvania Avenue, bordered by H Street above that, and by Madison Place and Jackson Place on the east and west. When the White House was first built, the park was meant to serve as an "outdoor lobby," a kind of grand reception hall. Later, Pennsylvania Avenue separated the White House Lawn from Lafayette Square, and the land became a park. By this time, the park was surrounded by the residences of people seeking influential positions with the Executive Branch.

"These were powerful people, with big egos," Calarco explains. "So there were lots of duels and murders. The people who died often had unfinished business." As our tour group strolls the perimeter of the park on a cool August evening, she spins stories of old war heroes, former presidents, and that famous First Lady, Dolley Madison—each of them maintaining a residence of sorts on their old stomping grounds.

One of the more amusing episodes Calarco recites features General Daniel Sickles, a lawyer, New York Congressman, and Civil War hero. An extraordinarily colorful character, Sickles' story involves a late marriage to a much younger woman, her affair with a family friend, and Sickles' homicidal revenge. Both Sickles and his murder victim, Philip Barton Key (son of National Anthem author Frances Scott Key), have been sighted as phantoms in the area. During the Battle of Gettysburg (well after the murder and subsequent trial), Sickles lost his leg when a cannonball crushed it. That didn't bother him so much. He donated it to the Army Medical Museum, and visited it every year on the anniversary of the amputation, July 2, even after he was dead. You can see his leg for yourself—as well as the cannonball that took it—at the National Museum of Health and Medicine (NMHM), on the Walter Reed Army Base in Northwest Washington (see the article on the NMHM in this book). One of the telltale signs of Sickles' ghost is a trail of cigar smoke, so stay alert as you walk through the park.

Another celebrity ghost, Commodore Stephen Decatur, survived the War of 1812 as a naval hero, but later died in his home on the park after a duel with Commodore James Barron. The tour relates the story of how these old friends came to pistol shots on the dueling grounds of Bladensburg, Maryland, just north of Washington. Decatur's ghost may just be an excuse for Calarco to recount the pertinent history of his accomplishments, but she is able to dispel rumors about the mysteriously bricked-in windows of his house at the corner of H and 13th Streets. Some have said the windows were covered to prevent the ghost from making street side appearances.

Stephen Decatur may still be visiting his former home today, says Carolyn Crouch, Founder of Washington Walks and creator of the company's ghost tours. She recalls a young man on her tour three years ago who told of his father's odd encounter while attending a black tie reception at the Decatur House. On his way up the stairs to the event, the father "was met coming down the stairs by a man dressed as if he was going to be fighting in the War of 1812. The father just assumed there was going to be a reenactor portraying Stephen Decatur at the party, or that maybe they had costumed servers with the catering company." But once upstairs, he noticed that the caterers were dressed in ordinary black jackets and ties, and the host said that he had not hired any reenactors. The father remains convinced he passed Decatur's ghost on the stairs.

"There's got to be something about that house," Crouch remarks, genuinely amazed. "Because the Octagon has more varied ghost stories associated with it, but in terms of recent things that people have experienced, the Decatur House has more. The woman who's the director of public programs [at Decatur House] right now has experienced two things that she told me about."

Crouch started Washington Walks in 1999 to supplement her income as an actress. She had been on several walking tours in London, noting "that was the best way to get a really intimate look at the city and find out a lot in a short time." Returning to Washington, she couldn't find a comparable company to work for...so she started her own. The first year, she only gave one walking tour, called "I've Got a Secret," which focuses on quirky trivia about the Nation's Capital. The following year, she added "Capital Hauntings," with "Most Haunted Houses" following the year after that. (The company now offers over a dozen specialty tours, including "In Fala's Footsteps," which covers history as seen by FDR's pet dog, and a snacking tour called "Moveable Feast.")

"We weren't even going to consider doing [a ghost tour] initially," Crouch says, "because I thought it would be too cheesy and silly." After taking a friend's suggestion and doing some research, she developed what instantly became her most popular walk. "When I created Capital Hauntings, I wanted it to be more about the history that produced the ghosts. For one thing, the ghost stories aren't that extensive. Sometimes those ghosts haven't done a lot of things," Crouch laughs. "But how they got to be ghosts is pretty fun to hear about."

The difference between the two ghost tours is simple. "Most Haunted Houses" focuses solely on homes, and at a slightly higher fee of $15 per person, you also get a tour of the Octagon. Both ghost tours cover the Decatur House and the White House, Crouch admits, "although we tell different stories at the White House." The haunted house walk also covers the Hay-Adams House (which once sat on the site now occupied by the hotel of the same name); and Major Rathbone's home on Jackson Place—naturally, Rathbone continues to stop there. "We talk about the Blair House, too," Crouch says, "which isn't haunted as far as we know, but we tell a story about why maybe it should be."

Crouch found the basis for her ghost stories in a book by John Alexander, currently available in a revised edition under the title *Ghosts: Washington Revisited*. These tales have been supplemented by information shared by her tour guests, other research, and lore related by staff at the Decatur House, the Octagon, and St. John's Church. However, one significantly ghost-ridden mansion was not forthcoming with information. "The White House visitor's center didn't want to talk about their haunted lore," Crouch notes. "I don't think they consider that an official part of the history of the building."

The reticence of the White House staff is unfortunate, for the place harbors numerous celebrity ghosts. As we stand in the middle of Lafayette Square Park during the tour, surrounded by a profound darkness, a full moon rises over us. The executive mansion glows weirdly under high intensity lights as if to scare away any supernatural visitors. Pointing out the statue of former President Andrew Jackson, Calarco tells us what she knows about the executive officers who refuse to leave their former residence: Jackson, who's known to stomp and swear; Kennedy, who appeared to LBJ; and Lincoln, who's manifested to quite a few of his successors, as well as to servants and the Queen of the Netherlands. Which just goes to show how democratically minded Honest Abe must have been.

Is it possible that Lincoln himself has instructed the current White House personnel to suppress information about him and his fellow Very Important Phantoms? In Washington's most haunted square, you never know.

Joseph Cornell Study Center

Smithsonian American Art Museum
750 9th St, NW
Washington, DC
(202) 275-1445
Website: www. americanart.si.edu/education/cappy/
13acornellbio.html
Hours: By appointment only; call at least 2 weeks in advance
Cost: Free

Deep inside the block-wide office building housing the Smithsonian's administrative offices, Elizabeth Anderson calls security. "I'm opening Room 31," she tells them, just before punching a secret code into a nearby keypad. As Collections Curatorial Coordinator for the Smithsonian American Art Museum (SAAM), Anderson is one of just a few who know the code. Once inside this small room, the special appointment, climate controls, and security measures seem like overkill. There are just shelves of large brown archival cartons here, after all. But for a fan of Surrealist artist Joseph Cornell, this is as close as anyone can get to the sanctum sanctorum of his basement studio on Utopia Parkway in Flushing, New York, where he created the mysterious shadow boxes that still haunt art museum goers today.

Anderson pulls down one of the cardboard cartons and removes the lid, revealing three wooden constructions packed side by side. Wearing rubber gloves to protect the object from the oils and acids in human skin, she carefully lifts one of the things out. It's a Cornell Box in embryo, the wood painted but not polished, just a couple strips of mirror glued to the inside wall, a small brass latch affixing the lid.

Had he lived, Cornell might have worked up this wooden rectangle into one of his meticulously crafted mini-museums filled with found objects, old photographs, and bottles of cryptic stuff. Anyone who's seen one of his boxes can't help but be captivated by their poetry. It's rare enough to see a completed Cornell box, so when I mention to friends that the SAAM houses what Cornell called his "spare parts department," they're usually eager to go. For Cornell fans, it's a bit like going to a garage sale at his house. You couldn't see all the stuff he never used if you had a million years, but you can ask for a glimpse of a few items in one of the 112 cartons—just to get a sense of his artistic process, you understand.

What kind of stuff are you going to see? There can be mundane things, like a box of cork balls, or marbles from a Chinese checkers game. Or more exciting things, like a pile of wooden birds Cornell made by gluing magazine pictures on a board and cutting around them with a band saw. As she's catalogued the collection, Anderson has seen it all. "I like looking at the white boxes from his studio," she says, her enthusiasm tempered by the tedium of an archivist's labors, and the special difficulties presented by all this flotsam. "I've found starfish, bird's nests, shells. There's just so much in there, such a variety of materials. Some of my favorite things to come across, I like the bird cut-outs on wood because that so clearly speaks to what's in his completed boxes. I like the wonderful Victorian cut-outs and stickers. He's got rubber stamps that he used. There's a box that just has compasses in it. I just enjoy opening up that box and seeing all the compasses in there jiggling around, their needles going in different directions."

Anderson opens another carton and pulls out a few treasures for me to see. The first thing is an old cigar box painted white; the "El Producto" logo is still visible through the whitewash, and on the side, in blue paint, Cornell has scrawled, "Tin Foil." And that's exactly what's inside—a thick stack of it. A whitewashed tea tin labeled "Penny arcade, (Birds) Pegs" contains dozens of wooden pegs from an unknown old game, saved for one of Cornell's series of boxes that he called "Penny Arcades." Colorful postage stamps in many shapes fill a flat box, dozens of clock hands are jumbled in another, and a third small box opens to reveal a smaller box, which opens to reveal—nothing. It's empty!

Here's an intriguing item: a manila envelope—addressed to Cornell himself—containing "b' flies," according to Cornell's own note. That must mean "butterflies," because the artist has stashed hundreds of carefully trimmed color images of these and other insects. Alongside this, Anderson pulls out a bundle of old newspaper, tied with a string. "This is one of the things that freaks me out," she says, a little mildly for someone clearly surprised by what she's holding. "I don't know who bundled them, but I swear no one has looked at them—ever. They're yellowing. They're from 1972!"

So Cornell was a pack rat. But when you think like he did of the myriad possibilities behind these simple objects, you begin to realize that this isn't somebody's "trash," but a window on the cosmos itself. Such was the transformative power of Cornell's genius.

The Cornell Study Center was established at SAAM in 1978, when Cornell's sister, Elizabeth Benton, donated these spare parts and his entire library of several thousand books to the museum. The deposit includes unfinished works and as many as 50,000 pieces of source material and studio effects. At least, that's a tally former Chief Curator Lynda Roscoe Hartigan once gave me. Anderson's still not sure how to add it all up. "Do you count each marble?" she asks rhetorically. "Do you count each piece of paper, or each file?" The museum's Archives of American Art houses Cornell's diaries, correspondence, and other papers. In all, it's an astonishing record of Cornell's exploratory process of gathering, sorting, and sifting through materials to create a body of work that's considered a new art form.

By the time of his death in 1972, his collections had spilled out of the basement to overtake the whole house. Cornell imagined the place becoming "a home museum and/or experimental workshop," where visitors could explore their own dreams using the materials he had accumulated. Don't get too excited. The Cornell Study Center is not meant to be a realization of that dream. Instead, it's kept mostly as a resource for scholars. Cornell lovers are allowed brief visits—with an appointment made two weeks in advance. But even the most die-hard aficionado may be perplexed—disturbed, even—by some revelations that are best left to the Ph.D.s.

"Here's a weird one," Anderson notes wryly, opening a book-sized tan box inscribed "Mouse Material" to reveal a bed of dark gray fuzz. "What this is, I have no idea. It's like cotton wool, but it's just filthy!"

This little object is nothing less than a hidden artwork that Surrealism's guru Andre Breton would have loved. I mean, a box labeled "Mouse Material" and filled with dust bunnies? That's incredible! It's the ultimate Duchampian prank!

Since you can't exactly specify what you want to see (unless you're a bona fide academic conducting "research"), visiting the Cornell Study Center can be a bit like playing the lottery. You never know what's going to turn up. At least here, every surprise is a winner. It's your chance to visit Cornell's studio—and help him complete his thoughts on where these objects were going. As with his boxes, understanding this material starts with your own memories.

Drug Enforcement Agency Museum and Visitor's Center

700 Army Navy Dr., Arlington, VA
(202) 307-3463
Website: www.usdoj.gov/dea/deamuseum
Hours: Tues-Fri 10 a.m.-4 p.m.
Cost: Free

You may feel it's a little creepy dropping by the Drug Enforcement Agency (DEA) Museum—especially if you enter through the wrong doors. If you use the DEA's main entrance, a man in a black suit and tie is sure to approach and quietly ask if he can "help" you. Don't panic. You're not here to turn in your bongs and rolling papers, right? So he'll merely instruct you on how to get to the Hayes Street entrance around the corner. You'll find the correct door marked by a nifty full-color sign featuring a large opium poppy. It's a weird image for the DEA to use as a calling card, but a lot of things about this museum seem contradictory.

The museum opens on a triptych portraying the history of America's love of, er, experience with drugs. On the far right: a 1930s drug store, where cocaine and heroin were readily and legally available in all kinds of products, from teething cures for baby to Bayer brand heroin and cocaine-laced Coca-Cola (the rumors are true!). Next, the 1970s, represented by a giant photo of a mustachioed head-shop proprietor proudly grinning over the biggest water pipe you've ever seen. "Those were the days," as Edith Bunker used to sing. Finally, a steel crack house door, "circa 1990s," is mysteriously set into the wall. Look through the door's Plexiglas window to view a giant photo of two little kids scrambling to pick up used crack vials. Notice the progression from peaceful, small-town America to violent, urban wasteland America? In between, the establishment of prohibition, enforcement, and the DEA. What are they trying to tell us?

Move along to the permanent exhibit, "Illegal Drugs in America: A Modern History," which expands upon the triptych's theme. In the beginning (apparently), there were Chinese immigrants, and they brought opium with them. Between the 1840s and 1914, these drugs filtered into the middle class, as heroin, opium, and other drugs were increasingly used in patent medicines, hysteria cures, treatment for injured Civil War soldiers—and for entertainment. Plexiglas cases overflow with silver opium pipes and other paraphernalia (a very popular word in this museum),

73

antique medicine bottles, and giant hypodermics. The walls are papered with photos of young women shooting up. Weapons come on the scene starting with the passage of the first drug laws in 1875 (in San Francisco, of all places) and the foundation of the first Bureau of Narcotics. From here, displays alternate between sensational images and news clippings of drug use, and the increasingly heavy armory and more sophisticated investigation techniques of the drug police.

So the fun begins. Jazzbos, hipsters, and beatniks are chased by G-men and hysterical pop culture makers across the walls and display boxes of the exhibit hall. Charlie Parker, Mezz Mezzrow (he introduced marijuana to the jazz scene!), Lady Day, Jack Kerouac, Allen Ginsberg, Tim Leary, William S. Burroughs, and Albert Hoffman (inventor of LSD!) are pictured and name checked, while pulp paperbacks (1950's *Quartet in H*) and movie posters (1957's *The Pusher*) rise in the background. The counterculture has begun—and so have the drug wars. The psychedelic era is predictably eye-popping. The DEA could open up a real head shop with all this confiscated loot: a wall full of homemade, improvised, and store bought pipes; colorful rolling paper packages; bongs; and a hilariously futuristic "marijuana intensifier" that looks like something out of Woody Allen's *Sleeper*.

Things don't get out of hand until you hit the G-man's undercover garb. First, a pair of green snakeskin shoes worn to infiltrate the 1970s band biz in Detroit. (Band unnamed. Bets, anyone?) Then there's the "Superfly look." Yes, we've entered nose candy land: sniffing spoons and failed smuggling techniques proliferate. Did someone really think a hollowed out surfboard would get past customs?

Enter the 1980s, and things get scary. The G-men are wearing riot gear and packing serious artillery, the stakes are higher, and the photos—including documentation of Columbian Cartel violence—are bloodier. The meth trade and the crack wars aren't colorful and silly and creative. What you get is people busting down your door. We have entered "The DEA Today." What's up with that?

The large room at the end of the hall is reserved for changing exhibits; when they've finished here, they go on tour. If you miss the current display, "DEA: Air, Land & Sea," the museum may be bringing confiscated Sea-Doos and drag racers (once owned by real drug lords) and a real DEA helicopter to your hometown. And budding entrepreneurs won't want to miss the detailed exhibits on how to construct a real meth lab (both "Nazi" AND "Red Phosphorus" methods!). The lobby displays preview upcoming exhibits on Club Drugs (I'll bet you always wondered why ravers carried pacifiers and soap bubbles and Pez dispensers), cannabis, and the "rainbow drugs" craze of the 1970s. A motorcycle formerly owned by a Hell's Angel when he dealt drugs on the mean streets of Salem, Massachusetts, is parked in the lobby. Plus, you can explore DEA "career opportunities" and case studies on interactive computers.

There's even a gift shop, so you can stock up on coffee mugs, t-shirts, and drug-related books. They also have plush eagles and teddy bears wearing little DEA logo shirts for family members that may want to smuggle drug money, uh, I mean, remember their encounters with the DEA. And don't miss the "DEA mini badge set" of lapel pins "representing previous agency badges." But remember: no impersonations of officers!

Despite the bureaucratic stuffiness and high-school-health-class style deadly seriousness of it all, the DEA Museum is a thorough, informative, and fascinating document of America's Dionysian excesses—and its attempts to stifle them—since the nineteenth century.

Exorcist Stairs

From Prospect Street and 36th Street, NW, down to M
Street, NW, near Key Bridge
Georgetown, Washington, DC
Hours: All hours of the day and night
Cost: Free

Officially known as the Hitchcock Steps, this flight of seventy-five slate steps and three landings was made famous as the scene of two violent deaths in the 1973 horror film *The Exorcist*. Bordered by a stone wall on one side and the outer brick wall of the Car Barn on the other, the steps lead from an M Street gas station to the Georgetown University campus. These stairs may be one of DC's pop culture landmarks, but they're not particularly special unless you're looking for exercise. Today, Hoya athletes often "run the stairs"—the equivalent of a five story building—for a rigorous workout. And it's a campus tradition to screen the movie every Halloween.

In the opening of the film, the camera pans across the Key Bridge, showing M Street, the main artery of Washington's Georgetown neighborhood, with Georgetown's distinctive buildings sitting above it all on a hill. It focuses in on the stairs, with a gas station at the bottom and a series of townhouses at the top. This scene remains virtually unchanged today. A residential property at the top of the stairs (owned at the time by Mrs. Florence Mahoney) was used only for the exterior shots of the house where actress Chris MacNeil (played by Ellen Burstyn) and her daughter Regan (Linda Blair) are staying. The way the film is edited, it looks as if Regan's bedroom window looks out directly over the stairs, allowing for Father Karras (Jason Miller) to leap out the window to his death. In reality, the house sits about thirty feet away from the head of the stairs. To make the house appear closer, a special false addition was added—a walls-only facade that allowed sunlight to enter Mrs. Mahoney's garden.

Today, the view of the house from the stairs is partially obscured by a privacy fence and holly trees, though from the front you can see it's a narrow brick townhouse. You get a better view of the property from the deck of the Car Barn, a huge academic building housing the McDonough School of Business (back when Georgetown still had street cars, they turned around on the ground floor of the building). If you're interested, scenes from *The Exorcist* were also filmed on campus at the Healey Building, Old North, Quadrangle, the track, and Dahlgren Chapel.

When William Peter Blatty was writing his novel *The Exorcist* in 1969, he relied on familiar territory to provide the setting and inspiration for the book and, later, the screenplay, which he also wrote. He was living near the top of the Hitchcock Steps, at 3618 Prospect Street, very close to his alma mater (he was in Georgetown's Class of '49. After graduation, Blatty transferred to George Washington University, also in the city, where he earned a master's degree in English Literature.) While still an undergrad, Blatty read a *Washington Post* article about a case of demonic possession in a local fourteen-year-old boy. This much is part of the well documented lore of the book and film. According to the article, the possessed boy lived in the Washington suburb of Mt. Ranier, Maryland, at 3210 Bunker Hill Road. Don't bother looking for the house. First of all, that property was razed long ago. Second, it wasn't the possessed boy's home, anyway.

Historian Mark Opsasnick has determined that the possessed boy of the 1949 article actually lived in a different suburb near Mt. Ranier, called Cottage City. The house is 3807 40th Avenue. A small, one-story, single family home, this setting for the original exorcist story—the real one—isn't scary or unusual in any way. Instead of trekking out there, read Opsasnick's report of his fascinating investigation on his website: www. capitolrock.com.

The stairs aren't particularly scary, either, unless you're afraid of heights. At least from the top of the Hitchcock Steps you get a grand view of the C&O Canal, Potomac River, and the Rosslyn, Virginia, skyline.

Gargoyle Tour

Washington National Cathedral
Massachusetts & Wisconsin Avenues, NW
Washington, DC
(202) 537-6207
Website: www.nationalcathedral.org/cathedral
Hours: Fourth Sunday of the month at 2 p.m., Apr-Oct
Cost: $5

Are you ready to go big game hunting in the wilds of DC's embassy country? The Washington National Cathedral offers thrills no wilderness safari can provide—but leave your blunderbuss at home. The only tool you'll need is a pair of binoculars. Can you spot the three-headed dog? The unicorn? The hippie? The beatnik rabbit wearing a beret and holding a paintbrush? How about the dentist kneeling on a walrus' stomach to clean the creature's tusks? Score as many sightings as you like. When you're hunting beasts made of stone, there are no time limits, no quotas, and no way to scare them off!

One of the world's newest cathedrals (completed in 1990), the Washington National Cathedral has some of the world's newest and funkiest gargoyles. Of course, there are the usual dragons and flying hybrid beasts, but most of them are based on equally fantastic ideas (for a gargoyle, that is), like the businessman, the artist, the bishop, the birdwatcher, the sculptors themselves, and the "Devilish Gardener"—all rendered as outlandish caricatures. You're invited to play "spot the gargoyle" anytime, but on the fourth Sunday of the month from April to October, there's a more formal expedition that starts with a lecture and slide show, which reveals some carvings you'd never otherwise see. Then you tramp around outside with your eyes following a knowledgeable finger pointing skyward at the highlights. It's just about the most fun you'll ever have in or around a church!

With 112 gargoyles to search for, you could be craning your neck at the cathedral walls all day. Some are easier to find than others. Fairly low on the North Nave wall, you can readily spot the "American Rattlesnake," twin serpents coiled around a log; the "Sleek Dragon;" and a basenji, otherwise known as the "African Dog." On the Northwest Tower, you might find the "Administrator," a four-armed, three-eyed humanoid with his glasses askew, clutching a model of the National Cathedral School for Girls. This gargoyle was designed by Norman Rockwell's son, Peter, and carved by an unknown craftsman. Peter Rockwell designed eight gargoyles in all for the cathedral, including the rather chauvinistic "Woman Unmasked," an ugly woman who reveals her true nature, and "Egg," an odd creature emerging from an Easter egg and wielding a brush to paint the designs on its own shell. For sheer weirdness, no gargoyle tops the numerous winged reptiles, griffins, and mythological figures like the skeleton with a snake curled in its skull. The serpent enters the skeleton's left eye socket, winds its body in the cranium, and pokes its head out the back of the skull. Ominously titled "Decay," this figure can be spotted on the second level of gargoyles on the South Nave, near the South Transept.

The Washington National Cathedral was built from east to west, starting in 1910 and continuing to 1990. (It's officially known as the Cathedral Church of Saint Peter and Saint Paul, but all their materials use the shorter moniker.) Because the foundation stone was laid in 1907, it's generally considered that construction took eighty-three years, an estimate which includes long breaks in the work due to lack of funds. The first architect of the cathedral, Henry Vaughan, omitted grotesques from the earliest sections of the building—that is, the apse and the North Transept—because he adhered to a simpler, twelfth century form of Gothic design. He may have felt the gargoyles interrupted the upward sweep of the cathedral, getting in the way of the visitor's view of God. Vaughan had a point, because in later Gothic style, "Each time there's an intersection of lines, there's a carving to break that starkness, to soften the cathedral," reveals docent Miles Moore on a recent tour. A fifteen-year veteran tour guide with the cathedral, Moore was one of the first docents to give tours that focused exclusively on the gargoyles. (Before 1998, gargoyles were only covered briefly during other specialty tours, and then as the occasional focus of the "Tea and Tour" program.)

The first gargoyles began appearing in the early 1960s as the South Transept was erected, but gargoyle production didn't kick off in earnest until the main phase of the cathedral's construction, from the late 1960s to 1977. During this time, Roger Morigi served as Master Carver for the cathedral, guiding the creation of niche sculptures, crockets (the little balls you see on the tower spires), and angels, as well as gargoyles and other grotesques.

The significance of Morigi's tenure at the cathedral explains why the tour guides make a big deal about the bizarre caricature of him that appears on the North Nave. Because of his explosive temper, the other carvers called Morigi "The Walking Devil." As Moore explains, "If any of his stone carvers made a mistake, he would practically take the cathedral apart stone by stone." This terrible view of him is reflected in his gargoyle's features, some of which are true to life. Morigi really did have a perennial five o'clock shadow and always wore an old cloth cap. But his grotesque likeness (called "Master Carver") also has things its sculptor, John Guarente, only imagined, like a little atomic mushroom cloud spouting from his head, a curled devil's tail, a dagger, and a pistol.

Morigi is just one of the carvers immortalized in stone. His successor, Master Carver Vincent Palumbo, is represented as a grotesque winking and whistling at the school girls who passed as he worked on the cathedral walls. Paired with him is a likeness of the dean, his mouth agape and hat askew, clearly shocked by Palumbo's lechery. Both figures face the National Cathedral School for Girls, across Woodley Road from the cathedral. Yet another Master Carver (and Morigi's precursor), Joseph Ratti, is represented as a grotesque. Because he died from a fall during construction, the other artisans left two uncarved blocks at the base corners of a North Nave gablet in place of carved figures, a symbol of the work Ratti would never do.

What's the difference between a gargoyle and a grotesque, you ask? Well, the name "grotesques" indicates the larger family of uglified or whimsical carvings that appear on a cathedral. Carvings called grotesques are usually smaller than gargoyles, and serve solely as decoration. (There are 1,130 grotesques—not counting gargoyles—on the Washington National Cathedral, and they can be equally worthy of hunting. A few grotesques are discussed on the tour.) While all gargoyles are considered grotesques, they are distinguished by the important work they do; that is, each gargoyle is a drain spout helping to carry rainwater runoff from the cathedral's acre and a half of roof away from the walls. The water flows through a pipe in the center of the carving, to emerge from the gargoyle's mouth. But unless you arrive in a thunderstorm, don't expect to see the gargoyles in action. "I've seen a gargoyle spit just once," Moore notes helpfully, "when workmen poured a bucket of water through it."

The design of the gargoyle has changed over the centuries to improve this drainage function. "In the Middle Ages, they couldn't carve a hole through the stone," Moore points out, "so they just put a groove down the gargoyle's back. We have two in this manner." One is a rabbit, the other a dog. "Nobody can tell me exactly why," she adds, "if there was something wrong with the stone, or if they just wanted to do it in the French way." Anyone who loves gargoyles knows that they were supposed to scare evil spirits away from the holy edifice—but it appears the principle danger may be the elements, particularly rain, which can damage stone and mortar, thus weakening the walls.

One might think that the gargoyles are freestanding sculptures, like the replicas commonly available in garden stores or museum gift shops, but such construction would create problems in attaching them to the walls. So just how do the gargoyles stay in place? "The gargoyle's not just stuck up there with chewing gum," Moore jokes. "The back half is the wall." Indeed, the stone carver actually worked with a long, rectangular block of limestone, only half of which would be shaped into the gargoyle. The other half of the block remained square—literally forming part of the cathedral's structure. That's why grotesques are considered architectural carvings, rather than ornamental. The Indiana oolitic limestone used throughout the cathedral is a soft material with an even grain that allows for easy carving and a finely textured finish. It has the added properties of hardening as it ages in the open air, and of retaining an elasticity that allows it to expand and contract in response to weather changes without breaking.

The wide-ranging subject matter and often whimsical designs of the gargoyles reflect the cathedral's ecumenical nature; though affiliated with the Episcopal Church, the cathedral welcomes all points of view. A case in point—in gargoyle terms—would be the "Hippie," a true relic of the 1970s, the period in which he was carved. Moore gives the run down on his features: "Torn shirt, loaf of bread, carrying his protest sign, and between his feet, a bag of marijuana," before joking about the last item, "See if you can find it." The figure also has a large trumpet strapped on his back. This feature was intended to be a drain, but the pipe was never connected. "We call it a wannabe," Moore reports, reminding us that true gargoyles are fully functional drainspouts. Perhaps this is a commentary on the hippie's work-refusing lifestyle.

Another of the most popular carvings is also a secular fixture of pop culture. As soon as Moore announces that Darth Vader's face appears as a grotesque high on the Northwest Tower, everyone begins craning necks, pointing fingers, and popping eyeballs to find him. In a few minutes—and with a pair of binoculars helpfully passed out by the docents—everyone is satisfied. "For those of you who are Star Wars fans, this is the dark side of the building, the North side," Moore jokes, referring to the direction of the sun's rays, not the Force. Darth is one of four winners of the Draw-a-Grotesque contest, held in 1985 and sponsored by the children's magazine *National Geographic World*. The Dark Lord shares a gablet with another contest winner, a perky raccoon.

But no cathedral would be properly dressed without a classic winged reptilian gargoyle, and the Washington National Cathedral has plenty to scare off tradition-minded malevolence. One of the cutest of these, "Refusing to Listen," covers his ears with his little hands. Moore interprets the figure as "evil refusing to hear the word of God." Evil or not, the recalcitrant little fellow is represented as a stuffed toy in your choice of red or green plush in the cathedral's extensive bookstore and gift shop. He's one of numerous gargoyle-related souvenirs the cathedral has manufactured in recent times, including a series of resin figurines, a postcard book, and an excellent *Guide to Gargoyles and Other Grotesques* that should prove essential to any enthusiast. That guide—plus a good pair of binoculars and a camera with a big, big lens—should help you bag the best gargoyle trophies on your cathedral safari. Happy hunting!

George Washington Masonic National Memorial

101 Callahan Dr.
Alexandria, VA
(703) 683-2007
Website: www.gwmemorial.org
Hours: 9 a.m.-4 p.m. daily
Cost: Free

From its lofty position on top of Shooter's Hill, the George Washington Masonic National Memorial rises high above the city of Alexandria, Virginia, just across the Potomac River from Washington, DC. You can't help but wonder what's inside—even if you're not obsessed with the role of Freemasonry in every conspiracy theory ever devised. But you won't need a secret knock or password to visit. You don't even have to be a brother. Just drop by. A tour guide will meet you in the grand foyer, usher you into a crazy Wonka-style elevator that actually rises at a 7.5 degree angle into the building's tower, and open the doors to room after room decorated in a different manner: an Egyptian tomb, Solomon's palace, and a medieval castle. The place is crammed with Masonic memorabilia, plus loot of broader historical interest. If that's not enough, be patient. An awesome view of the Potomac and the surrounding metropolis awaits!

The George Washington Masonic National Memorial was first conceived as a fireproof repository for an impressive collection of George Washington's personal artifacts and other Masonic items that the Alexandria-Washington Lodge had been collecting since Mrs. Washington's death in 1802. Architect Harvey Wiley Corbett took inspiration from ancient beacon towers, like the legendary lighthouse at Alexandria (the ancient Egyptian city) that was one of the Seven Wonders of the World. This choice was clearly symbolic, meant to express the sentiment that Masonry had been a guiding light to General Washington, just as he was a guiding light to his nation. When it was completed in 1932, the 333-foot tall building must have seemed gargantuan; today, the memorial still towers over the massive office buildings, apartments, and hotels that have sprouted up nearby. It will always be a model of neo-classical architecture, with its central portico supported by six columns and the majestic tower built of stepped blocks, topped by a stepped pyramid.

To enter the building, you pass through the the portico and into the magnificent Memorial Hall. A seventeen foot tall bronze statue of Washington in Masonic garb greets you as your eyes follow the green marble columns into the fifty-one foot high ceiling. Echoes swirl mysteriously through the room. Two giant murals depicting Washington at official duties stretch the length of the room, one on each side, halfway between floor and ceiling. Above them, six stained glass windows depict colonial era statesmen like Franklin, Jefferson—and, of course, Washington himself. The murals and windows here and throughout the building were painted by Allyn Cox, muralist for the U.S. Capitol and a master of many styles to fit the moods of these symbol-minded Freemasons.

While you wait for an on-the-hour foray into the upper floors, you're welcome to explore the main level in a self-guided tour that includes views of two lodge meeting halls and adjoining exhibition rooms. The exhibits feature an intriguing variety of Masonic bric-a-brac, including Masonic razors from 1910, ceremonial trowels, photos, trophies, and medals galore, even Mexican General Santa Anna's spurs. The story goes that when captured, Santa Anna saved his own life by flashing the Masonic distress symbol to his guards and Texas General Sam Houston. Another odd souvenir is the pair of handcuffs John Brown wore prior to his execution, retained by the Alexandria-Washington Lodge member who escorted Brown to the gallows.

When a scheduled tour begins, the guide—and that Wonkavator— will take you to nine of the eleven floors in turn. Before your conspiracy radar goes haywire, Jim Williams, a guide on a recent tour, assures me that the tenth floor is reserved for ham radio equipment (very likely), and the eleventh is a "filthy, dirty attic I don't have any desire to see." (Wow! Imagine the possibilities!) First stop, the George Washington Museum, said to contain the "most outstanding Washington memorabilia to be displayed to the public." I'm no judge of that, but the scrimshaw whale's tooth with a portrait of George Washington is pretty cool. There are also two locks of Washington's hair, a key to the Bastille presented by Lafayette, and a pillowcase quilted from Masonic ribbons. Plus, the antique Masonic aprons painted with weird glyphs and emblems are amazing pieces of folk art.

The next several floors are dedicated to different branches of the York Rite Masons. The Royal Arch Masons' room is decorated like an ancient Egyptian tomb, with paintings of Egyptian and Hebraic masons performing trade related activities: carrying a keystone, squaring blocks, preserving the Arc of the Covenant. These murals are rendered in a faux-Egyptian style, with the figures strikingly outlined in black, and they represent a remarkable deviation from Cox's more realistic style on display elsewhere. Most stunning of all is the image of a fantastic, four-winged angel rising out of a burning bush to address Moses. On one side of the room is a painting of the ruins of Solomon's temple. The opposite side contains a screened off alcove; at the end of the pre-recorded narration, the curtain opens for about twenty seconds, revealing "the most beautiful reproduction of the Arc of the Covenant ever created for Masonic purposes"!

Then there's the Cryptic Room, replicating a vault below Solomon's Temple and featuring exquisite Cox pictures in Pre-Raphaelite style, not to mention the only blacklight mural in the world! Above that, the Knights Templar room, home to two suits of armor. Perhaps the highlights here are four tall stained glass windows that stretch high overhead; these portray the life of Jesus in jeweled colors and heroic images. Williams claims that no meetings or ceremonies occur above the second floor—except in this room, where young men "do part of their investiture," and the occasional wedding takes place.

Next is the Tall Cedars room, dominated by a replica of Solomon's throne. From here, a door opens to the outside, looking down the long stretch of King Street, Alexandria's main artery, to the Potomac River 430 feet below. Step onto a narrow observation deck guarded by a cage of metal grillwork to see the most magnificent view of Washington and the surrounding metropolis this side of the river. Follow the Potomac off to your left, and the Washington Monument, Capitol, and Jefferson Memorial are clearly visible, as is the Washington National Cathedral farther to your left and slightly behind the building. Somewhere between here and the ground are a few floors we haven't seen, but who's counting? This king's eye view seems to be the Mason's real secret—and it's one they're quite willing to share.

Giant Mermaid

Lee Highway
Arlington, VA
Hours: Anytime
Cost: Free

Who says mermaids don't exist? Anyone looking for proof positive need only drive down Route 29 in Arlington, heading East away from the East Falls Church Metro station. Look to your right between Potomac and Powhatan Streets and you'll see her rising eighteen feet out of the lawn of a Mediterranean-style white house. High and dry in the suburbs, this giant mermaid may be a bit out of her element. (The nearest body of water deep enough for her to swim in—the Potomac River—is a few miles away.) But her ecstatic posture, arms raised and outstretched to embrace the house, tells you she's found her home.

From the street you get a profile view of the mermaid's long arms, the stream of hair flowing down her back past her waist, and her scale-covered tail curled up behind her. She releases a dove from her left hand, and an angel fish and a sea horse rest at her tail fin. Close observers will not fail to notice that the lady is particularly well endowed. In fact, with her blond mane, rounded derriere, and huge breasts, the mermaid looks like she was designed by filmmaker Russ Meyer as a tribute to Chesty Morgan.

"If any sailor ever dreamed of a mermaid, I'm sure he would want one that looked like mine," says Paul Jackson, the mermaid's proud owner and principal designer.

The mermaid was originally an eighty-five foot tall white ash, "about six foot in diameter at the base," Jackson says. Estimated to be 130 years old, the tree had been growing nearly three decades when the house was built. In their own twenty years of residency, while Paul worked for the DC Fire Department, retired, and started a paint contracting business, and Nancy taught high school English, the Jacksons came to view the tree as a "fixture of the house." They felt it balanced the large trees on the other side of their yard and provided a delightfully shady canopy. Naturally, they were crushed when the tree took sick—possibly the result of routine tree work to thin the crown, a measure to prevent wind strain on the trunk.

The Jacksons had seen tree stump sculptures as they passed through Lancaster, Pennsylvania, on the way to Nancy's hometown near Philadelphia. "They do a lot of tree carving up there: eagles, bears. Nothing really unique, but I always liked the carvings," Jackson says. "When we lost the tree, I said, 'I'd like to get the tree carved.' So I had it cut off at about twenty feet." Nancy found Frederick, Maryland-based carver Scott Dustin on the Internet, and together, the three decided on a tribute to Paul's love of beautiful women and the water. "I love fishing; I love sea life," Jackson admits, noting that he specified all the mermaid's features, from the dove in her left hand, to her hairstyle and the angel fish at her side. The sea horse was a concession to Nancy's interest in those animals. The mermaid's face and hair were based on an Italian cast bronze sculpture Jackson owns. "I love the long flowing hair," Jackson notes. "[Dustin] did very well."

As for those breasts, you can thank (or blame, as the case may be) Paul. "When it came to the time of the boobs, the sculptor said 'How big do you want 'em?'," Jackson recalls. "I said, 'As big as you can get! Double-D sounds great to me.' You got a big girl here. She's got to have breasts, right? So he got Double-D's for me, and they'll never need silicone, either, 'cause they'll never drop."

The artist was a little surprised at the final size of the mermaid's bustline, however. "In fact, when I started making it, I told them, 'I don't think she's going to have much of a chest at all,'" Scott Dustin reveals. "The intent was to have the hair over the front. When you're creating a subjective sculpture, you always leave extra so that you can take away, 'cause once you cut away too much, there's no putting it back. The size they are now is the size that I left them with the intent of having hair over her breasts. So they changed their minds and said that's fine. Had I put the hair over them, they would be more realistic looking."

Dustin is pleased with the way the whole sculpture turned out, but he does like one part better than the others. "My favorite part of doing it was her torso area," he says. "Because to me that's the most sensual part of a woman, below the chest down, just because men aren't built like that. Women have a stomach and hips that to me are just really sexy."

The only things Dustin would change are the large hands—although practical concerns dictated their size. "If you carve things too small and too long, they'll be too fragile," Dustin explains, "I was afraid that if I made the hands more ladylike, that because it is a log, and it will dry and crack some, something might happen to them down the road." Still, Dustin is able to justify the result in biological terms. "As far as the hands go, obviously this is a mythological creature," he says, "and my way of thinking is that if there is a real mermaid or merman, they're gonna have some awful powerful arms and hands to help them get through the water."

The mermaid project is the largest Dustin has ever undertaken in his seven years of carving, and it took him just over three weeks, or about 120 hours, to complete. He spared no pains in rendering the fine details of the facial features, waving hair, and fish scales. "He was very meticulous and slow, rather than whack, whack, whack," Jackson says. "He said, 'I could do a bear in a day,' that's what he told me."

The carving was carefully planned to prevent water damage; all edges are angled and there are no flat surfaces for water to collect on. Although white ash is a hardwood often used for ax handles and baseball bats, Jackson has taken no chances with his baby, either, laying on several coats of Sikkens wood preservative. "It's eighty dollars a gallon," Jackson notes. "She gets Sikkens for what I'm paying to have this done." The extra care has had an unexpected benefit. "It turned her into a strawberry blond, too," Jackson reports. "I like that. It's a beautiful wood. You can see the grains in it."

Dustin started carving from the top of the tree in order to control the proportions of the sculpture. Working on an eighteen inch diameter branch, the first thing he carved was the dove and the mermaid's left hand. "You had a trunk here with a dove and a big hand," Jackson recalls. "I come out here about seven in the morning, there were three old ladies praying to the dove of peace! The ladies thought it was spiritual. That's fine with me. I wanted to have something like [the mermaid] was reaching to God." He couldn't be more pleased with their tribute, taking it as a good omen. "The tree was blessed from the inception," Jackson says, somewhat awed. "I guess she'll be there a long time."

The creation of the mermaid was a daily revelation for the Jacksons. "It was neat to leave in the morning and come home and say, 'Oh, look what he's done now!'" They snapped photos of the entire process, from the carving of the dove's outstretched wings to the seaside-style landscaping around the sculpture's base. Nancy has taken to calling the mermaid "D.G." "It's an acronym for 'damaged goods,'" Paul explains. "She says the tree was damaged, and we turned her into perfect goods."

Interestingly enough, Jackson prefers to gaze upon this perfection from a distance. "The view I like is when I walk across the street, where you get to see her hair and the sea horse and just enough of the bosom that gets you interested," he admits. "It's just gorgeous when you look at her that way. From the street you get a nice, beautiful view of the artwork. And with the boulders around there and the sea grass blowing, you get an ocean scene, and it looks like she's coming out of the water. You think every time you come home you're going to your beach house!"

Jackson is perfectly willing to share his newfound view of paradise. Twenty cars stopped for a look during the short time of our interview, and he estimates that 200 to 300 people pause to view the mermaid each day.

Jackson extends an open invitation to them all. "Enjoy her," he declares. "That's the purpose of her, or I wouldn't have done it in the first place. I really enjoy people enjoying her. I consider her art, and I love art. If all these people enjoy it, I feel I've done something good for Arlington County."

Gold Rush DC: Catching Gold Fever in Great Falls

Great Falls Tavern Visitor's Center
C&O Canal National Historical Park
11710 MacArthur Blvd.
Potomac, MD 20854
(301) 767-3714
Website: www.nps.gov/choh
Hours: Daily 9 a.m.-5 p.m.
Cost: Free

On the trail to the Maryland Mine above Great Falls and the C&O Canal, the freshly fallen leaves rattle underfoot so loudly I can barely hear my guide, Ranger Rod Sauter, pointing out the signs of gold excavation hidden in the terrain. The Gold Mine Loop trail leads up the hill above historic Great Falls Tavern through thick woods of majestic tulip poplars, young American beech, and skinny pawpaws. Although mining stopped long ago—the work simply was not profitable enough to continue—visitors to the park can experience gold fever just by viewing the mill ruins and other mining features in C&O Canal National Historical Park.

"This is one of the main Maryland mining sites, and one of the most easily observed and accessible mining sites in the park," notes Sauter, Supervisory Park Ranger for the park's Great Falls Interpretive District. Every year, Sauter leads an interpretive hike from the Great Falls Tavern up to the mining site. But don't worry if you've missed it; the trail is always open for self-guided trips to the mining ruins, and the Tavern Visitor's Center houses a small display on the mining activity here.

Legend has it that a Union soldier camped near Great Falls, Maryland, was washing dishes when he saw gold flecks sparkling in the stream. His discovery jump-started a miniature East Coast gold rush that resulted in thirty small mines spread across the hills of Montgomery County, Maryland, above the falls. The remains of two other mines, the Ford and the Anderson, are also within park boundaries. This activity rekindled an industry that in Maryland is as old as 1829, according to Walter Goetz's booklet "Montgomery County Gold Fever" (available in the Tavern gift shop).

The first of the new mines, the Maryland Mining Company, was founded by former Union soldiers in 1865. The next year, the Maryland

Mine began to produce actual gold, and the Union Arch Mine was founded in the surrounding area, near what is now the Cabin John Aqueduct Bridge (then known as the Union Arch). Over the following decades, mining occurred sporadically on the Maryland Mine site, as one company gave up and another was infected with gold fever. The hike follows the path of this history as it moves uphill from the tavern just over a mile to the mine ruins; the round trip takes about two hours. Less ambitious gold enthusiasts may take a five minute shortcut down the Falls Road Spur, a trail near the intersection of MacArthur Boulevard and Falls Road at the park's edge.

Off the trail and up a hill, we spot one of the first landmarks, a long ridge of earth—now covered over in leaves—that clearly isn't nature's landscaping. A closer look reveals a two foot deep prospecting trench dug from east to west in order to locate the vein of quartz running north-south; the quartz vein is represented on the current topography by a groove that perpendicularly crosses that prospecting trench. During World War I, the Atlantic Development Company spent $130,000 on this excavation. The mysterious work back in the woods caused locals to suspect that a German invasion force was digging trenches in the hills, and federal authorities were called in to investigate. Today, small chunks of quartz poke up from the leaf cover; these chunks are the remains of mining activity. Some larger pieces further down the hill may have naturally broken through the soil with erosion, Sauter says; these quartz boulders, or "floats," would have signaled the nearby vein.

Further up the hill, we come to our first mine shaft, originally dug in 1867. The shaft was filled in years ago for safety reasons; these days, it's just a giant indentation lined with leaves, and a mature tree grows from the center of the bowl. Nearby and enclosed in tall chain link fence, lies a jumbled pile of rusted, corrugated sheet metal. After a moment's study, it's not hard to see it once was a rather large structure that collapsed almost half a century ago. This ruin was a crushing mill, built in 1935 by yet another Maryland Mining Company when gold prices rose to $35 per ounce. Here, quartz rock was broken into successively smaller chunks in preparation for amalgamation, in which the crushed quartz sand was washed over a copper plate coated in mercury. The mercury combined with the gold, forming an amalgam that stuck to the copper.

Near the mill lies ruins of other company buildings. The assay office and water tower have been reconstructed, but are protected by tall chain-link fences and signage offering stern warnings of the dangers of hidden mine shafts and rickety construction. Underground and unseen lie three or four mine shafts up to 200 feet deep, and horizontal tunnels, called "adits" in the trade, that were dug along the quartz veins. This last Maryland

Mining Company worked the area until 1940. There has been no mining activity on the site since then.

Sauter can't help but compare all that effort and expense to the total gold recovery from all the Montgomery County mines from 1860 to 1951: a mere 5,000 ounces. At today's price of about $277.80 per troy ounce, that's $1,389,000 worth, although historical payouts totaled only $150,000.

"Gold digging is literally a scheme to get rich quick," Sauter says. "But if you look at the effort put in here, it definitely wasn't a way to get rich quick. The challenge was to find where the gold was and how to get it out. It was just too expensive." Over time, he adds, "the land itself became more valuable, especially being underdeveloped land in a highly developed area."

Before I have a chance to ask, Sauter quickly notes that mining and panning for gold is no longer allowed here: "The gold deposits are protected by the park."

That fact, and the knowledge of poor financial returns doesn't discourage most people, however. "I tell people about all the effort involved in prospecting," Sauter says, "but when I ask them if they would still do it, they say 'Yeah!'"

The Holy Land of America

Franciscan Monastery and Church of Mt. St. Sepulcher
1400 Quincy St., NE
Washington, DC
(202) 526-6800
Website: www.pressroom.com/~franciscan
Tours daily on the hour 1-4 p.m.; M-Sat 9-11 a.m.
Cost: $1 donation

The Holy Land of America is a real monastery and a real church staffed by real monks, but the faithful replicas of holy shrines in Jordan, Israel, Egypt, and Syria are, well, fakes—which makes this unique attraction a little like Vacation Bible School and a little like Disneyland. The purpose is serious, though. The reproductions highlight the Catholic Church's centuries old mission for the Franciscan Order: that is, guarding and preserving the Holy Land and other (real) shrines of the Christian faith. But don't let that deter you if you're not seeking divine inspiration. It's worth a visit just to see the replica Roman catacombs and the Purgatory Chapel, with its mosaics of resurrecting skeletons and saints' tombs. Both are delightfully spooky. In a holy way, of course.

The building project started when Father Godfrey Schilling immigrated from Germany to construct a shrine that would educate people about significant Biblical landmarks in the Holy Land. "There were no airplanes at the time; you had to go by ship," notes Father Kevin Treston, Pilgrimage Director at the church today. "Father Godfrey's dream was that people who could not go to the Holy Land, for financial or medical reasons or whatever, they could see some reproductions of holy places in the Holy Land and the catacombs of Rome."

Once ground was broken in 1896 at the abandoned McCeeny estate, the church was finished in two years and dedicated in 1899. In 1897, Schilling was joined by a group of six other Franciscan monks called the "Pioneer Brothers." Together, they renovated the grounds of the run-down twenty acre farm, cultivating the gardens and growing vegetables. When the complex was finished, it included a monastery, the Church of Mount Saint Sepulcher, and the replica grottoes outside; eventually, it became known as the Holy Land of America. The naming may be confusing, but the purpose is simple, Father Kevin explains: "You see, we're not a parish church, we're a shrine, like the National Shrine." Although people of other faiths come here and are welcome, he says, "it's mainly to teach the

Catholic faith to our people through picture and image. It's a catechetical tool is what it is, but in full size. We're a shrine church. We do have masses and confession for the people, but that's just a service we supply. There is no other place like this anywhere in the U.S."

Today, the grounds are a physical and spiritual refuge from the hectic pace of urban life surrounding them. The gardens are rightfully famous for their roses and the cultivated wildness of the mix of native woodland plants. These sloping plots of camellias, azalias, bee balm, buddelias, and towering magnolia, cedar, and hemlock trees dramatically descend into a valley where several replica monuments await. The view of this valley from the Rosary Portico is one of the most beautiful scenes in the city. You could even call it, um, heavenly!

Here, you'll find New World versions of the grottoes of Gethsemane and Lourdes, and the tomb of the Virgin Mary, lovingly constructed of concrete poured over wire forms. They sound hollow if you knock on the walls, but a feeling of mystery nonetheless pervades these underground retreats. Statues of saints and smaller flower gardens surround the area.

At the top of the hill, you enter the church through heavy doors near the gift shop to wait for tours which start on the hour. The anteroom is well-stocked with relics—both real and reproduced—including ceremonial cloaks, and a large collection of crosses and boxes in-laid with mother of pearl. A smaller glass case contains numerous intriguing artifacts, including a crown made of thorns from the Holy Land, a facsimile of a Roman nail used in crucifixions, oil lamps, and glass vials of water from the Jordan River. Among these items are two pottery firebombs from the Crusades (one has been burst open, presumably exploded), and a bronze amulet once worn by a dancing girl in the Roman period.

Your tour guide wears a special white uniform marking him as a member of the Knights of Mount Saint Sepulcher, a special order created by Father Schilling to aid the monks with the Holy Land of America tours. He will introduce you to the numerous altars and chapels of the church and explain their relationships to Holy Land sites. Often, fascinating trivia emerges tangentially from the recital. On a recent trip, I learned that the bas relief panels behind St. Anthony's altar were based on live models. Rev. Schilling himself makes an appearance in the leftmost image—as the penitent on crutches!

After covering the altars, the tour follows the highlights of the Easter story, including the Crucifixion scene at Mt. Cavalry, a replica of Jesus's tomb (also known as the Holy Sepulcher), and the Resurrection. While the church itself is not as dramatic as the nearby Basilica of the National Shrine of the Immaculate Conception, it is strikingly beautiful—and very much like visiting any historical Catholic church—with pews, corner chapels laden with candles, and a towering pulpit—although this one has more elaborate visual aids.

The best is yet to come as the tour descends into a replica of Roman catacombs. From the trompe l'oeil stone blocks at the entry way to the tunnels lined with burial niches and saints' remains, the catacombs are a spooky wonderland that would be the highlight of any Halloween mansion. After a quick stop at the Nazareth Grotto, commemorating the Immaculate Conception, a few paces takes you deep into the catacombs of Rome. Along the walls, there's an inset chapel honoring St. Benignus, a Roman general beheaded for his Christian beliefs. "The Romans would behead their citizens," Father Kevin explains, "while crucifixion was reserved for foreigners." Resting on a slab of white marble above a marble rendering of a reclining Roman officer, there's a two foot tall, glass-fronted box that seems a bit out of place here. In a building full of "fakes," this box contains the general's genuine remains.

"These were given to Father Godfrey Schilling when he built the church," Father Kevin notes, "given to him by a bishop from outside Rome. But the bishop did not give him the skull piece, which was kept by the bishop in his church for veneration. So we have everything but the skull piece; if you look inside the little box you'll see ribs and ulnas and arm pieces."

Yet another genuine relic lies in these passages: the remains of St. Innocent, another early Christian martyr who was killed with his family. "Those are actual remains, not a copy," Father Kevin says, "given to us by the friars of the Sacred Heart Providence, who had those in a boys' school in Oak Brook, Illinois, outside Chicago. The face is a mask, it's not real. Underneath is a skull piece, of course. The hands and the feet are real; they look mummified now, but those are the actual feet. The black coloring on the hands is gold gauze that tarnished. We didn't touch anything. That glass casket came to us as it is. We put the second pane of glass on the front so people wouldn't tap on it."

You haven't seen anything until you reach the Chapel of Purgatory, lined with mosaics depicting the angels of Life and Death, Jesus raising Lazarus to life, and the burial of the dead, all rendered by long forgotten Italian artisans. None of these images tops the horror, the weirdness—or the humor—of the wall-length picture of nearly life-size skeletons rising from the dead at the end of time. Their grinning faces leer into the room, gleefully inviting the visitor to join their party. After all, it is supposed to be a happy occasion! "The raising of the dry bones, that's a vision Ezekiel had—it never happened," Father Kevin explains. "It's a vision representing the Jews coming back to God and resurrecting as a new people. It's symbolic of new life."

"The Purgatory Chapel is just to teach people about purgatory," Father Kevin adds quickly. "There are no catacombs like that in the Holy Land or in Rome. [Those are] just here to teach a lesson about the faith."

The final stop is an exact reproduction of the catacombs of St. Calistos, a pope who gathered the remains of many martyrs and buried them in one place. This copy is complete with simple, cartoon-like murals of Biblical stories, just like the real catacombs in Rome. "There's Susanna and the Elders, the Last Supper, all these things are there according to the image of the people of that day," Father Kevin says. "Noah's Ark is my favorite; it just looks like a man in a box." He points out one problem with faking it: "The originals are frescoes, which last for ages and ages. Ours are just paintings, so ours can fade and have to be redone."

When you re-emerge into the brightly lit chapel, you may wonder whether this is supposed to be a replica of resurrection. But you're not finished yet. No tour of religious reproductions is complete without a trip to the well-stocked gift shop, offering postcards, kitschy plastic icons, and a bin of tin medallions for fifty cents each, but the Garden Tour pamphlet is the only essential. You'll want any excuse to roam those garden paths again. Let the city wait.

International Spy Museum

800 F St., NW
Washington, DC
1-866-SPY-MUSEUM; (202) EYE-SPY-U
Website: www.spymuseum.org
Hours: 10 a.m.-5 p.m. November-March; 10 a.m.-7 p.m.
April-October
Cost: Adults: $13; Seniors (65+), Active Duty Military,
Intelligence Community: $12; Children age 5-18: $10;
Children under age 5: Free

An old saying recommends that if life gives you lemons, then make lemonade. Here in Washington, life (OK, the government) has given us the CIA, NSA, and FBI, not to mention rogues like Aldrich Ames and Robert Hanssen, turning the city into a playground of geopolitical intrigue. Over the years, various "Spy Tours" have attempted to create excitement out of formerly chalk-marked mailboxes and clandestine meeting places. But not until the International Spy Museum came along has anybody applied lemonade logic to such great effect, taking DC's spy legacy and turning it into something truly thrilling. The best part is that the museum doesn't rely on suspension of disbelief to make you wonder at the mysteries of espionage exploits. On the contrary, from the moment you pay the rather steep admission fee, you begin an odyssey that's way more Universal Studios Tour than Smithsonian. From the start, the museum builds a mysterious atmosphere, as flashing walkway lights lead you to the elevator that will carry you deeper into the building, and an overhead female voice with a British accent warns, "Please watch your step. Remember, we'll be watching you!" Once inside, you feel like you're IN a movie, but it's not a James Bond adventure. This is more like *The Matrix*.

In the "Covers and Legends" room, a man appears on multiple overhead television screens insisting that you carefully create an alias from the examples on the walls and pillars around the room. "Be prepared to live your cover!" he advises. This is creepy fun with a purpose. The displays lining the walls show the types of documents real agents use to create a false identity and fictional biography. Well, it can't be that simple, but you get the idea. You can test your memory of your new identity at interactive computer displays sprinkled throughout the museum, and at the "final checkpoint" at the end of the tour.

When Big Brother tells you to move to the "Briefing Room," follow the crowd quickly or you'll be locked in the alias area forever! You're about to see a film cut at MTV speed that describes why people become spies and what they do. It's heavy on Cold War history, but it features a titillating sound bite from a former KGB head who intones, "There are more spies in Washington, DC, than any other place." And now we have the museum to prove it!

The International Spy Museum opened in July 2002 as "the only public museum in the United States solely dedicated to the trade craft, history, and contemporary role of espionage." It purports to display the largest collection of international spy artifacts EVER (which turns out to be "over 600"). As you roam through hall after hall you're certainly likely to agree. No one room seems especially loaded with goodies, but there sure are a lot of rooms, each covering a different aspect of spy history from biblical times to the present.

The museum's building itself is a kind of "museum of buildings." The outer structure integrates five nineteenth century office buildings from the old F Street corridor, including the Warder-Atlas Building (built in 1892), the Le Droit Building (1875), 812 F Street (1875), the Adams Building (1878), and 818 F Street (1881). Each of these historic structures have their own history. The Warder-Atlas Building once served as U.S. Communist Party headquarters, and the Le Droit Building was developed by a co-founder of Howard University. The Spy Museum fills the facade created by these fine examples of Romanesque Revival and Italianate architecture. The new complex includes two restaurants (Spy City Cafe and Zola), a gift shop, event space, and museum offices. The museum itself occupies only the first and third floors of the block-wide building.

The tour gets into more traditional, "show and tell" exhibits in the "School for Spies" section. Here, younger kids crawl through large ducts overhead while their elders watch short how-to films on bugging and lock-picking. Notice the sign warning you that "Someone is Watching" (probably some kid in the ductwork) and the large chrome fly on the wall (get it?). Traditional glass case displays share glimpses of many varieties of secret radios—including a *Get Smart!* style shoe with a heel transmitter, dead drops, and containers with concealed compartments, microdots, tiny cameras, and World War II era escape tools. Check out the umbrella gun! Look, off in the corner, it's a silver Aston Martin DB5 just like James Bond used in *Goldfinger*! And above that, a short training film on sabotage! Play "find the mannequin cam" as you watch yourself on an overhead TV! These geegaws can be so entertaining, you quickly forget that real spying is actually tedious—and dangerous—work.

Pay close attention to that Aston Martin. Bond himself wouldn't know the difference, as it's been tricked out to completely replicate the movie version (which was destroyed during filming). First of all, the license plate rotates through several ID tags, including "007," but that's just the beginning. "It also has a rotating disc with knife-like protrusions on the rear axle of the driver's side, so that if someone is trying to run [the car] off the road, that would shred their tires," notes Peter Earnest, founding Executive Director of the International Spy Museum. "Some people might like to have that on the Beltway!" he quips, adding, "There's also a bulletproof shield that rises out of the trunk area and covers the back window. In the exhibit, you hear the sound of bullets firing, and clearly they can't get through because of the shield. Finally, there are two covers in the front headlight area that drop down and reveal machine guns. Lights flash and sounds are made like automatic weapons fire from those."

Next up, "The Secret History of History," where you'll trace the "second oldest profession" from the Trojan Horse to Renaissance courts and Japanese ninjas. It covers early cryptography, but if you're really serious about this aspect of spycraft, you'll head over to the National Cryptologic Museum in Ft. Meade, Maryland (see the article on it in this book). Just to spice things up, there's a giant pin-up photo of Mata Hari in houri garb, alongside a genuine letter she wrote and signed. [The Spy Museum knows what it's about: down in the gift shop, Mata Hari postcards are more expensive than any others.] And don't miss the little alcove reserved for the museum's weirdest exhibit: a little stuffed bird in a Plexiglas case wearing a box camera strapped to his chest. It's the pigeon cam!

"He looks like a little American tourist in Paris," Earnest jokes before detailing the giant leap for spy-kind at work here. An ingenious combination of ancient and modern technology, the pigeon cam takes advantage of the bird's natural homing instinct, which was used successfully by the Romans, and the time-release shutter camera, developed around World War I. As the bird flew back to its roost, the camera automatically snapped multiple shots of the ground below. An example of one pigeon's handiwork appears on the floor and one wall of the room. You can even see the feathers at the pictures' edges!

"If you look at it in the broad picture of man's interest in and development of technology to spy on his fellow man, [the pigeon cam] in effect is the beginnings of overhead reconnaissance," Earnest explains. "You start with the pigeon, and you eventually get to the Wright brothers, then to sending planes such as the SR-71 and the U2 high up into the air. Eventually, you get to that enormous technological breakthrough of the

Cold War, and that was the development of geosynchronous satellites. In some ways, it all began with the pigeon."

But once you pass through the "Doorway to Hell," the museum's tone changes considerably. This door is none other than the disguised entrance to Moscow's notorious Butyrka Prison, where Soviet dissidents were "interrogated" during the early days after the Revolution. These themes are continued in the next section, "Spies Among Us," which covers World War II code-breaking and disinformation, and the chain of espionage from Pearl Harbor to D-day. From here, it's a straight shot to pure, unadulterated A-bomb hysteria! Welcome to the atomic spy room, where an ominous, overhead narrator (Big Brother again) lectures on the dangerous link between Soviet spies and American traitors who stole atomic secrets from the Manhattan Project. Throwing subtlety to the wind, the exhibit graphically demonstrates what could have happened. Cue atomic testing, complete with countdown, flashing lights, and shaking floor!

After you catch your breath, you'll stumble down two flights of stairs into a fallout shelter. The walls are lined with sandbags and posters from Red Scare films and other propaganda. So goes the "War of the Spies," where the Cold War is new again, with your celebrity hosts Ethel and Julius Rosenberg! This may be what hell is really like: wandering a maze of chain link fencing, while clips from the McCarthy hearings blare overhead. You descend into a replica of the Berlin tunnels used as a base for U.S. spies to monitor Soviet communications, and from there to an extensive exhibit on spying in Berlin during the Cold War, aerial surveillance, and stories of more recent double agents in the U.S. and the Soviet Union.

Set off in a small theater, an on-screen ex-KGB agent—retired Major General Oleg Kalugin—lectures on these efforts to cross and double-cross. An early reformer of the KGB, Kalugin was elected to the Soviet Parliament during Gorbachev's Glasnost era. Since emigrating to the U.S., Kalugin has become a professor at the Centre for Counterintelligence and Security Studies (CI Centre) in Alexandria, Virginia, and is currently a member of the Spy Museum's Advisory Board. (Kalugin also participates as a tour guide on "The Spy Drive," a "'classroom on wheels' journey" around DC's espionage highlights. These tours are just one offering by a CI Centre offshoot called SpyTrek. Check their tour offerings on the web at www.spytrek.com.)

Earnest reveals that he and Kalugin have become friends, and remarks drily, "He and I have occasionally done things in tandem. That is, having a former KGB officer and a former CIA officer together brings a certain set of atmospherics to any occasion." Undoubtedly, the two can swap many a yarn about relations within and between superpowers—which would make attending their joint presentations at the museum essential.

The final stop is a large screening room where a film called *Ground Truth* relentlessly reels out the most emotionally charged highlights of guerilla warfare and terrorism in the twentieth century, from Pearl Harbor, to Honduras, Afghanistan, and 9/11. The soundtrack is an angelic piece of choral music sung by a Bulgarian women's choir (straight from the *Mystere de Voix Bulgares* album!)—as if these news clips weren't heart-wrenching enough. A Big Brother voice intones, "The irony of our time is that terrorists and international criminals are using our technology against us. More technology hasn't made us more safe, it's made us more vulnerable."

But isn't that an exceptionally heavy way to end an amusement park ride, uh, I mean a museum tour?

"The film is an attempt to look into the next century," Earnest explains. "In other words, as we tour the museum, what are the things to come? The purpose is not to be pessimistic or optimistic, but to fulfill the mandate of intelligence, which is to reflect the world as it is, not as we would like it to be. I think it's one of the best summaries of what we're dealing with, with net warfare, and up against these groups that are described in the film."

It's a short walk—but a long emotional and intellectual leap—from that clip reel to the museum gift shop. Is it really a good marketing strategy to depress people before you let them loose on your t-shirts, coffee mugs, keychains, and postcards (each in at least a dozen different designs!), spy related books, DVD movies, tools, toys, and a novelty grocery money hiding place disguised as a peanut butter jar? Um, can you say "retail therapy"?

Sadly, what's not on sale are the cool vintage spy toys and movie memorabilia sprinkled through the heavy stuff at historically appropriate moments. Like the copious collection of tin police and G-Man cars and toy pistols from the 1930s and 1940s, plus all kinds of mint-in-box spy kits. Just look at that tin machine gun. Death was never so colorful!

There's also a section on celebrity spies, like Julia Child (who only worked in a war office), Josephine Baker, and baseball star Moe Berg, near a simulated 1930s movie theater playing segments from Donald Duck war propaganda films and espionage-related movies. Further along the halls, there's an alcove where a giant TV plays clips featuring every supersleuth from Bullwinkle to Austin Powers as you drool over a pile of rare loot from the classic 1960s TV and film heroes like James Bond, *Get Smart*, *Dragnet*, *The Avengers*, and *The Man from U.N.C.L.E.*

I saved mention of these pop culture goodies until last just to end on a positive tone. But it's a testament to the International Spy Museum that you're not likely to remember these items unless you took notes. The museum makes the real gadgets, the real heroes and villains, the real dangers, consequences, successes, and failures—that is, the REAL stories of REAL espionage—so exciting that you're more likely to think you're on a rollercoaster than in a museum. A trip to the International Spy Museum is one wild ride through history.

Johnston's Garage D'Art

Johnston Auto Paint and Body
8137 Lee Highway, Merrifield, VA
(703) 560-1226
Viewing hours: Anytime
Cost: Free

If I'm lucky, the light will turn red for me at the corner of Gallows Road and Lee Highway in Merrifield, Virginia. I love revisiting the lawn ornaments and primitive paintings on the old building sprawling on the southeast corner. There's the lawn jockey pointing the way to the Beltway exit, the rooster weather vane, and the naive painting of a blacksmith handing a little girl a newly made wagon wheel. I no longer have to look at the sign above the sprawl of painting bays and the maze of skinned and dented cars on its impossibly tiny front lot to know that I'm at Johnston's Auto Paint and Body Works. Then the light changes, and the traffic carries me away.

Edward Johnston, Sr., bought the building in 1963 and began sprinkling it with objects around 1972. Over the years, there's been a pair of cement lions guarding the front porch, a decayed bull head, an eagle roughly carved from a log, and four Cavaliers, in red and blue, protecting the rear corners of the building with broken swords from peaked balustrades. You never know what you'll see peeking out of an odd cranny—or what will be missing the next time you pass. Although Mr. Johnston passed away in August 1996, many of the original decorations remain, neglected but impassive observers of the busy scenes of the business and the roadway.

The paintings were commissioned by Johnston from shopworker Kena Ruffner in the earlier days of the decorating. They're all done in a primitive, folk art style, and feature flat, spray-painted backgrounds and images supplemented by wooden cutouts of the major figures. Among the paintings, there's one with a wooden cutout of a horse-drawn covered wagon crossing a spray-painted desert while two cutout Indians watch from a painted hill. Another features a cutout Indian shooting a wooden buffalo with an arrow from horseback (the buffalo is now missing), and painted volcanoes rising in the background. Yet another has cutouts of four soldiers on horseback roping a bear with real string in a painted forest.

"He had everybody working on this place," shopworker Marty Turner tells me, as we stand in the tiny front lot. Marty's a veteran of over thirty years at the shop who clearly relishes his surroundings; I've seen him

113

working on the roadside lot and waving at passing cars. "They make you as crazy as this place," he says playfully of the decorations. "Mr. Johnston just wanted to make it look different."

"I've always liked toys, animals, decorations since I was a kid," Johnston told me once, when I sought him out to learn more about his homemade monument. He recalled one Christmas when he was twelve and no one in his neighborhood could afford Christmas presents. "I went to this warehouse that had a lot of toys. They'd left the back door open, and I filled a bag with toys. It allowed me to play Santa for all the kids." This generosity and knack for entertaining came back to him once he settled on the shop's present location. "I just put up whatever stuck in my mind," he said. "They say 'Once a man, twice a child.'"

Johnston's son, Edward, Jr., who has managed the shop since his father's retirement in 1990, recalls a more studious approach to the ornamentation. "He used to look at all kinds of architecture books, and if he decided he liked a certain thing, it went up," he says, referring to the rippling stone wall beside the front bay and a since-disassembled waterwheel. "He pretty much did it himself. He did what he felt like doing."

Many figures and several larger features have been lost to weather and road construction. When Gallows Road was widened in 1970, the lot was reduced by 600 square feet, which meant the waterwheel and a heavily decorated front porch had to go.

Items blown over or broken in storms have been removed and not replaced because the planned expansion of Lee Highway in the early 1990s put the entire building in jeopardy. "They're still talking, but we're still here," Johnston, Jr., said in 2001. "We put a new roof on and did a little painting here and there. But we haven't done anything with the decorations. All that stuff costs money and time. We've wanted to make money more than that."

The sad truth is that the artwork and the building are decaying, and every year there are fewer items on the building. But Johnston, Jr., has no plans to remove the decorations deliberately. "As [an item] gets old and deteriorates, we take it down so nobody gets hurt," he says. "I'm not interested in taking anything down and selling it or giving it away."

At the end of 2001, the paintings were removed so that repairs could be made to the building, and then replaced to their positions of glory, apparently after a good coating with weather-proofing varnish. They're now in a condition to last a while longer.

It's a good thing. An awful lot of people stop at those lights.

Brian MacKenzie Infoshop

1426 9th St., NW
Washington, DC 20001
(202) 986-0681
Website: www.dcinfoshop.org
Hours: Mon-Thurs 12-9 p.m.; Fri 12-10 p.m.; Sat 10 a.m.-10 p.m.; Sun 12-7 p.m.
Cost: Free

DC almost didn't get its own center for countercultural thought and action. "It's funny, if you look at the historical documents on the Infoshop," admits Wade, a volunteer at the MacKenzie Infoshop and one of the original collective members. "We have a lot of fliers and old bookmarks that say 'Opening in Fall '99,' and it's crossed out and written 'Summer 2000,' and that's crossed out and it says 'Winter 2001.' It's ridiculous! It got to the point where we told people we were finally opening, and they didn't believe us. They thought we were joking!"

Back in 1998, a small group of anarchist kids met at the Food for Thought restaurant in Dupont Circle to discuss how they could make the anarchist infoshop concept a reality in "the heart of the empire" (that's anarchist speak for you!). Before their second meeting, Food for Thought had closed. Their next two meeting spaces, both in Dupont Circle, also closed. It wasn't an auspicious beginning for any project, let alone a nonprofit, independent bookstore and clearinghouse for leftist politics and culture—they call it an infoshop—that depends heavily on community involvement and support.

But the infoshop collective was determined. Several of the group were also members of Positive Force, DC's venerable organization of social activists that grew up with harDCore (that's "DC Hardcore" for those who never heard the punk band Minor Threat) in the 1980s, so they'd not only learned some old school perseverance, they also had the blessings of the established group. Positive Force even held a few fundraisers for the infoshop when it lived a nomadic existence, setting up tables at punk shows, conferences, protests, or anywhere else they were invited to sell radical books and music, and distribute free zines (self-published magazines), pamphlets, and fliers.

"For five years before the store opened, the Brian MacKenzie Infoshop did very much exist in theory, and occasionally in practice," notes Wade, by way of explaining the delays in opening. We both agree that it's probably best not to use his last name in these days of the Patriot Act. "After our first year, we pretty much had the direction down. We looked for spaces for a bit, then we were invited to be a part of the Flemming Center operation. Then we were just subject to the ups and downs of their dealings with their contractors and construction workers."

All that uncertainty has become ancient history, however. "For us, it was never a doubt," Wade says confidently. "We knew we were going to open. We had the infrastructure set up, and when the building opened, we were one of the very first groups that were actually good to go. And we were fully open before most of the other groups had finished moving in. That's how much energy there was. We were waiting on this for a really long time."

The MacKenzie Infoshop hit the ground running on May 1, 2003, a date marked on anarchists' calendars as "May Day." (Usually known as Labor Day, May 1 marks the date of an 1886 resolution by the largely anarchist federation of American labor unions to adopt the eight-hour workday. The resolution sparked the Haymarket riots in Chicago and the execution of the anarchist union leaders. The history of this labor holiday—and the anarchist politics of the nineteenth century labor movement—is generally concealed in the U.S.) "We got lucky," Wade notes, "May Day being a big anarchist holiday—or *the* anarchist holiday."

And the shop has remained open long hours, seven days a week, thanks to the large pool of volunteers—as many as forty-five at this writing, with two replacing every one that moves on. Anyone familiar with "alternative businesses" is usually blown away by this regularity. "A lot of times stuff that doesn't take the shape of mainstream business gets seen as *ad hoc*," Wade says. "We want to be seen as very intentional and very conscientious about what we do."

That volunteer pool comprises the strength of the infoshop in more ways than one. For a store run as a nonprofit, by a collective in which everyone has an equal say in all decision making, the volunteers *are* the store. They determine what books and CDs to stock, what the hours and special events will be, and even the mood of the store during their individual shifts. Some volunteers have turned their hours into a party, luring visitors with free food or game nights.

DC's MacKenzie Infoshop is named after a young activist named Brian MacKenzie, an early collective member who had come to town for his freshman year at American University. For the first six months of his residency, he threw himself into the infoshop project, inspiring the other collective members with his energy and enthusiasm. In 1999, MacKenzie was staffing the infoshop's table at a punk show the collective had organized as a fundraiser when he had heart failure.

"Brian had grown up with a congenital heart defect, so he had a pacemaker and everything," Wade recalls. "I was working the door at the show. And a friend of mine came over and said, 'Hey, this guy's not looking too good.' When I walked back over there, he was on the floor. Some people jumped right in and performed CPR, did what they could, and called the ambulance. There wasn't a lot they could do, unfortunately."

MacKenzie's boundless enthusiasm for the project, coupled with his death on the job, sparked the other collective members to name the budding infoshop after him. And his parents blessed the project, too, diverting some donations given at their son's funeral to the start up fund. In a way, choosing MacKenzie's name over a catchier, more symbolic moniker (like Danbury, Connecticut's Mad Hatters Independent Media Center, or Philadelphia's Wooden Shoe infoshop, named after the *sabots* French factory workers threw into the machinery to stop production; the term "sabotage" comes from the name for these wooden shoes) was a way of defying the quirks of fate that seemed to be piling up against the project's realization. But more positively, it was a way of giving the budding infoshop a link to the contemporary anarchist scene—and thus to living ideas. "Infoshops have various names," Wade notes. "A lot of times they get named after anarchists of the past. There's a couple projects named after Emma Goldman; there's the Lucy Parsons Center in Boston. So [a name is] definitely a way of keeping those ideas alive."

Drop by the MacKenzie Infoshop on 9th Street between O and P Streets and you'll note that the tiny 350 square foot space is bursting with the energy of today's counterculture. Piles of free, small press zines, pamphlets, and fliers edge out from the main desk where a volunteer holds down the fort. Similar piles extend the magazine selection from a large rack to the floor. There are two shelves of mags like *Green Anarchy, Clamor, Anarcho-Syndicalist Review, Prison Index, Hip Mama,* and *Off Our Backs*; two shelves dedicated to zines that bear price tags, and four shelves of free publications. The zine titles alone signal the revolutionary bent of the shop: *Slingshot, Subliminal Criminal, Mother Rebel, Urban Hermit, Rice Harvester,* and *Critical Mass,* but these are only a small selection of the comix, personal diary-type zines, and collections of travel writings. The small section of CDs and LPs covers mostly punk and folk-punk music, but there are a few hip hop and experimental electronics albums. If you're looking for Beauty Pill, This Bike is a Pipe Bomb, Ghost Mice, or Against Me, they've got you covered. They also have albums by Phil Ochs and Woodie Guthrie, and Wade tells me these sell very well.

As the main focus of the shop, the book area occupies eight long shelves in the far corner. It's an eclectic selection encompassing graphic novels, poetry, sex, drugs, and punk, but it concentrates on anarchist philosophy, social activism, and protest movements, or "basically anything associated with radical politics that has an anti-capitalist or antiauthoritarian lean," Wade says. "We try to stock a wide range of things, but mostly stuff of an independent or DIY, meaning 'do-it-yourself' kind of ethic." You can also find books on animal rights, America's wars in the Middle East, and Black Liberation. They even offer the "Communist Manifesto"—but not works on the more authoritarian areas of communist or socialist party politics.

There's plenty more. *Beat the Heat: How to Handle Encounters with Law Enforcement* could be your "get out of jail free" card. *The Pornography of Meat*, by Carol J. Adams, analyzes the surreal associations between the meat industry and misogyny. Alexander Berkman's *Life of an Anarchist* could inspire your own. And the comic book entitled *Addicted to War: Why the US Can't Kick Militarism* may speak volumes about the post-literate generation's need for political consciousness raising. The shop's selection is rounded out by more "lifestyle" products: t-shirts, stickers, and the small table of alternative women's health products, like reusable tampons and speculum kits.

The books for sale share the corner with the free reading library, which encompasses a jumble of about 150 titles in subject areas paralleling the books and zines. That may not sound like many volumes, but when you realize that you can take your time with the sale books, too, then the whole place becomes a library of sorts. Space for hanging out to read is limited to a few chairs and the floor, but this hasn't stopped crowds from forming on evenings and weekends.

With so much free literature available in the place, you might not want to add to your pile of stuff with something you actually have to pay for—and that's the point, actually. "The amount of free stuff we carry is really important to us," Wade says, "to the extent that we'd like to have more overlap, so you pull a book off the shelf, or a CD or zine, and it actually says "Free" on it, rather than have a price. We've done that with a few things. We've hung t-shirts on the wall and put free signs on them, you know, nice new shirts. If we can get stuff for free, or donated, we'll do that sometimes. We really try to blur the line, and make people think differently about the function of a store. It just goes with our goal of providing resources to have a ton of free stuff."

The MacKenzie Infoshop occupies a small basement room in the Flemming Center, a space owned and partially occupied by Emmaus Services for the Aging, but the whole building—three old row houses converted into one unit—is activist friendly. Wade summarizes the role of the larger space with the enthusiasm of a guy who's really found his home. "Basically, the idea for the Flemming Center would be a mixture of progressive, social service organizations like Emmaus, that works with low-income senior citizens," Wade says, "and more grassroots or explicitly punk or anarchist organizations, like the infoshop, like the Washington Peace Center, which does grassroots peace organizing efforts, like Positive Force DC." The Positive Force offices are just around the corner from the infoshop, but that group's own library is on the second floor. Other groups in the building include the Gray Panthers, the Catholic Worker Bookstore, DC Books to Prisons Project, and the DC Independent Media Center. It's like a think tank for social responsibility! Wade crows about the numerous common spaces in the building, including a multipurpose room, a large conference room, and two kitchens. In one of the kitchens, the DC branch of Food Not Bombs cooks meals they serve for free elsewhere in the city.

Since opening in the Flemming Center space, the MacKenzie Infoshop has made good use of these extra rooms, hosting numerous readings, workshops, film screenings, and other events. A few days after the infoshop opened, Ariel Gore read from her published memoir about life as a punk mother and producer of *Hip Mama* zine. Other readers have included comedian and activist Robert Newman, and radical economist Doug Henwood. The collective has also sponsored several Zine Fairs to showcase the regional underground press; the one in 2003 was held in the Shiloh Baptist Church next door. During that event, the group offered a vegan Thanksgiving dinner, preparing food in both kitchens and serving in the multipurpose room. On their first anniversary, the infoshop held a day-long book giveaway and exchange, accompanied by a vegan barbecue lunch on the roof, an open mic for poets and musicians, and a presentation on the history of May Day. And on one July weekend in 2004, the shop sponsored three events: First, a teach-in for protesters attending the Republican National Convention. Next, a one-man play about globalization's effect on the African rainforest. Finally, Soft Skull Press graphic novelist Nate Powell and writer Josh McPhee (author of *Stencil Pirates: A Global Study of the Street Stencil*) did readings and signed copies of their books. To up the participatory ante, the infoshop also offered a how-to stenciling workshop and a "stencil swap," where artists could trade their designs.

While the infoshop idea may seem radical to those more used to the "ideology of bling bling" championed by chain stores and shopping malls, the MacKenzie Infoshop's nonprofit alternative seems to be finding its level in the neighborhood. An increasing number of locals drop by to check their e-mail on the free-access computer. "I've seen women come in with their grocery bags; it's like their route," Wade reports. "They do their grocery shopping, and they walk across the street to check their e-mail, and then walk home."

The concept, after all, isn't that hard to grasp, especially when it's so people friendly. "[An infoshop] serves as a place for people to meet other people, to leave fliers, to host events, to utilize for meeting space," Wade explains. "To have one place that serves as a focal point is really important. But DC really seemed like it lacked a location that was where it was at for activism, or anything of that nature. In any case, I meet so many more new people in DC just from volunteering once a week, because when people come in, this is where they go to get information. And it's not just to find out about protests. I've had people call the infoshop wondering where the nearest cooperative grocery store to their house was, or where they could get a used bike."

Wade sounds most pleased that the infoshop idea has really taken root in DC: "People just see the infoshop as a repository of information."

Mondo Mini Golf: A Guide to Mini Golfing at Night in the DC Area

When those DC summer days drag on with heat in the 90s and humidity through the roof, who wants to move—even to play a round of miniature golf? It's best to wait until sunset, when the air cools and fireflies light the edges of the green, before hitting the links. Most area mini golf courses have after dark hours and lighted ranges. Late hours also mean that even after school starts again you can keep up the par you've worked on all summer!

One of the most dramatic night mini golf courses is the one at Upton Hill Park, in Arlington, Virginia. A part of the Northern Virginia Park Authority, the Upton Hill course is arranged so that numbered greens work their way up and around a small hill. Waterfalls flow into an intricate system of waterways which run between the greens, forming water hazards in some places and emptying into ponds filled with water lilies and goldfish. The greens are skillfully designed for challenging shots. Standout holes include Hole 16, where the ball must go down a single hole into a giant funnel, and Hole 18, which involves three holes separated by undulations that drop the ball to a lower level. My 4-year-old son was able to turn both these challenges into holes-in-one for himself, but his mom and dad weren't so lucky.

But Upton Hill's *piece de resistance* is Hole 10, which features a green sloping 140 feet to the hole. Awesome. This hole used to be the "longest in the world" when the course was designed in 1990, but since then the mini golf course at Rocky Gorge Golf Fairway in Laurel, Maryland, beat them out with a 190 foot green!

Most courses in the area happen to be "resort style," which means an emphasis on landscaping and challenging green designs that mimic more serious, full-size ranges. Founded in 1964, Rocky Gorge is one glorious exception to the rule; among the garishly painted structures, you'll find "Needles the Singing Lonesome Pine," a singing cowboy, a model Washington Monument, and a clown with lighted eyes and a spinning nose. And do they get plenty of night duffers? You bet! "It's entertainment," Rocky Gorge owner Gus Novotny says. "We're competing with television, the movies, and everything."

Both Upton Hill and Rocky Gorge are lit by floodlights high overhead, keeping insects away from the golfers, with spotlights on key features. It may seem like you've found some extra daylight hidden over the greens, but the deeper shadows and cooler air give the courses an atmosphere of refreshing mystery. Whether beach or resort style, there are no colored lights to distract players. "The color comes from the place itself," Novotny says.

Another great "beach style" course for night golfing, Magic Putting Place, in Manassas, Virginia, has low lamps with colored plastic shades lighting each of its two courses, one dominated by a castle and the other by a windmill. Waterfalls descend from each structure into twin ponds with five spouting fountains. Cement geese, a saw mill, and a coal mine complete the scene. Greens are tough but unintentional challenges, as they slope away from the hole back to the tee, necessitating a gentle stroke.

The newest and most fantastic entry to the DC area's beach style line-up, "Perils of the Lost Jungle" at Woody's Golf Range in Herndon, Virginia, is themed like an Indiana Jones adventure. Golfers play through a jungle course, fending off animatronic alligators, snakes, natives, and more. The staff can even control some figures from behind the scenes, customizing each duffer's experience. So watch out when you get near the the poison arrow frogs—you never know when they might spray you!

With props designed by Advanced Animations, a company that has created mechanical figures for the Universal Studios theme park, "Lost Jungle" is a stroll-through adventure ride as well as a golf game. There's only one problem: this course is so packed with stuff (tiki heads, spiders, monkeys, etc), you may forget to putt.

There's no fooling yourself, however—you won't get to be Tiger Woods by staying out late on a school night fooling around with putters on oddly shaped greens. But take heart: Woody FitzHugh, a former touring PGA professional who now owns Woody's Golf Range (he's the principle visionary behind "Lost Jungle"), notes that "anytime you're putting at a hole, you're helping your golf game." That's good news for all mini golf - aholics dreaming of bigger things. Just be sure to use bug repellant to keep hungry mosquitoes at bay just as you're trying to sink a crucial putt.

Mini Golf Courses

The list below generally provides hours for the summer through Labor Day. Because hours change with the season, it's best to call or check websites for updated info. Prices are per person per game. Most locations offer group rates and birthday parties. Arrive at least 45 minutes before closing to allow enough playing time.

The District

East Potomac Mini Golf, East Potomac Golf Course, East Potomac Park at Hains Point, 972 Ohio Dr. SW. (202) 488-8087. Website: www.

golfdc.com/gc/ep/mini.htm. Hours: Open 10 a.m.-8 p.m. daily. Closes Oct 31. Cost: $4 weekdays; $4.50 weekends; ages 5-18 $3.75; group rates. Founded in the 1920s, making it one of the nation's longest running mini golf spots, the 18-hole course features multiple tiers, challenging tunnel shots, ponds with goldfish and water lilies, and a bridge. Plus, it's just a short walk to the Awakening Giant sculpture (see article in this book).

Maryland

Laurel Golf and Recreation, 9801 Fort Meade Dr. (Route 198), Laurel. (301) 725-4646. Website: www.laurelgolfcenter.com. Open 9 a.m.-10 p.m. daily; Sat & Sun 8 a.m.-10 p.m. Adults $4, children 12 and under $3. Streams run through this 18-hole, par-45 course, which features sand traps and a hole near a waterfall.

Rocky Gorge Golf Fairway, 8445 Old Columbia Rd., Laurel. (301) 725-0888. Open 9 a.m.-11 p.m. daily. $4 for unlimited play weekdays until 6 p.m., $6 per game after 6. The 19-hole, par-52 course claims their 190 foot green is "the world's longest mini golf hole." It also includes a singing evergreen tree called "Needles the Singing Lonesome Pine," a singing cowboy, a clown with a spinning nose and light-up eyes, the Washington Monument, a lighthouse, a train, and a wishing well.

Miniature Golf at Bohrer State Park (formerly Summit Hall Farm Park), 510 S. Frederick Ave., Gaithersburg. (301) 258-6420. Website: www.gaithersburgmd.gov. Open May-Oct with hours varying by season. Gaithersburg residents pay $4 per game, $5 unlimited play. Nonresidents pay $1 extra. The 18-hole, par-36 course has a waterfall and a garden pond.

Golfzilla Driving Range, 3601 Brinkley Rd., Temple Hills. (301) 630-4653. Website: www.golfzilla.com. Open all year: M-Sat 10 a.m.-9:30 p.m.; Sun 10 a.m.-8 p.m. $4 for ages 10 and up, $3 for ages 10 and under and 60 and over; under 3 free. The 18-hole, par-42 course may be flat, but it includes buildings, a windmill, and a cannon.

White Flint Golf Park, 5451 Marinelli Rd., Rockville. (301) 230-7117. Website: www.whiteflintgolfpark.com. Open all year, with hours changing by season. $5 for 8 and over, $3 for ages 4 to 7, under 4 free. Two 18-hole courses: North Course (par-43) and South Course (par-44) both include water hazards, roughs, and stone obstacles. A stream runs through the South Course.

Virginia

Cameron Run Regional Park, 4001 Eisenhower Ave., Alexandria. (703) 960-0767. Website: www.nvrpa.org/cameron.html. Open Apr-Oct: Summer hours M-Th 10 a.m.-9 p.m., F-Sun 10 a.m.-10 p.m. Reduced hours after Labor Day. $5.50 for adults, $4.50 for ages under 15 and over 60. The deluxe 18-hole course features sloping hillsides and a water garden.

Centreville Mini Golf & Games, 6206 Multiplex Dr., Centreville. (703) 502-7888. Open all year: Sun-Th 10:30 a.m.-10:30 p.m.; F-Sat 10 a.m.-11 p.m. $5.50 for ages 13 and over, $3.50 for ages 5 to 12, and $2 for ages under 5. The resort type 18-hole, par-42 course includes a downhill slope with water hazard on the eighth hole, ponds, and waterfalls.

Dulles Golf Center and Sports Park, 21593 Jesse Ct., Sterling. (703) 404-8800. Website: www.dullesgolfcenter.com. Open all year, hours change seasonally. $6 for adults, $5 for children ages 5 to 11. Ages 4 and under free. The 18-hole, par-46 course includes water fountains, stone traps, and waterfalls.

Fountainhead Regional Park, 10875 Hampton Rd., Fairfax Station. (703) 250-9124. Website: www.nvrpa.org/fountainhead.html. Open Mar-Nov 6 a.m.-9 p.m. $3.00 for all ages. Nothing fancy at this concrete 18-hole, par-36 course, but it's in a park next to Lake Occoquan.

Ironwood Sports Park, 8581 Cinder Bed Rd., Newington. (703) 339-3122. www.ironwoodsportspark.com. Open daily 9 a.m.-10 p.m. in summer. Adults $5.50; seniors and children 12 and under $4.50; under 5 free. 18 hole, par-41 course has undulations at each hole, waterfalls, and water hazards.

Jefferson Falls Miniature Golf Course, 7900 Lee Hwy., Falls Church. (703) 573-0444. Website: www.fairfaxcounty.gov/parks/minigolf/index.htm. Open Apr-Oct with seasonal hours. $6 for ages 13 and over, $5 for seniors and ages 12 and under, ages 2 and under free; group rates. The lushly landscaped 18-hole, par-36 course, accented by a bright blue waterfall at night, features tricky water hazards and contoured greens.

Locust Shade Park, 4701 Locust Shade Dr., Triangle. (703) 221-8579. Website: www.pwcparks.org/locust/locust_golf.html. Open spring to fall daily 10 a.m. to dark. $3 for adults, $2.50 for ages 3 to 17 and seniors 62 and over, under 3 free. 18-hole, par-48 course set in quiet, woodsy setting has different obstacles that require angle shots.

Magic Putting Place, 8902 Mathis Ave, Manassas. (703) 369-9299. Open spring to Oct daily 10:30 a.m.-10 p.m. until Labor Day. $3.50 until 6 p.m. M-F, $4.50 after 6 on weekdays and any time on Sat and Sun. Ages 3 and under free. Two 18-hole courses, each par-38, feature ponds, waterfalls descending from a castle and windmill, fountains, sawmill, and stable.

Upton Hill Regional Park, 6060 Wilson Blvd., Arlington. (703) 534-3437. Website: www.nvrpa.org/minigolfupton.html. Open Apr to Oct: M-Th 10 a.m.-9 p.m., F-Sun 10 a.m.-10 p.m. Hours change after Labor Day. $5.50 for adults, $4.50 for ages under 15 and over 60. Deluxe 18-hole, par-36 course runs around a terraced hill laced by waterfalls, streams, and lily ponds filled with goldfish. Challenges include awesome hole number 10 which slopes 140 feet.

Woody's Golf Range, 11801 Leesburg Pike, Herndon. (703) 430-8337. www.woodysgolf.com. Open all year: 8 a.m.-10 p.m. daily until Labor Day. Adults $8; 12 and under $6.50; under 5 free. Group rates. This themed course, called "Perils of the Lost Jungle," is built like an Indiana Jones adventure with loads of animatronic figures, snakes, natives, spiders, and shrunken heads. Oh, yeah, and there's a putt-putt course, too.

Mondo Mummies: A Guide to the Mummies of the DC Area

Mummies regularly get lots of screen time—from horror movies like "The Mummy Returns" to special television programs on the Learning Channel and the National Geographic series—but they rarely make live appearances. If you want to see mummies and learn about the mummification process up close, you'll have to do the visiting. We all love mummies for the same reasons filmmakers do—they're mysterious, creepy, ugly, and gross—in a good way that provokes curiosity about the lives these people led, and how and why they're still with us. This is your guide to the mummies in the Washington, DC, region.

Mummification is most commonly associated with the burial practices and religious beliefs of the Ancient Egyptians, who preserved bodies so that the spirits of the deceased could reinhabit them and live forever. The process of making a mummy was complicated, taking seventy days of exacting ritual and forensic practice. Methods varied, but generally mummifiers first removed the internal organs and placed them in canopic jars; the heart and liver were thought important, but the brain was not. The body was stuffed with linen, and sometimes sand and sawdust were placed under the skin to give a lifelike appearance. Next, the body was dried out with natron salts and rubbed with bitumen, or pitch, which sealed out moisture and gave the skin a blackened appearance. The classic Boris Karloff mummy always seems to have his legs free, but real mummies were wrapped completely in a cocoon of linen strips. Mummies were then placed in a coffin; the wealthiest clients sometimes were encased in two coffins and then the sarcophagus.

Although the Smithsonian's National Museum of Natural History has only one human mummy on display, he's actually something of a film star, being one of three mummies examined with computerized tomography (CAT) scans in a short film shown in the museum's Western Cultures hall. His name is "Minister Cox," and he's fully dressed in his bandages and a handsome gold face mask that includes a handlebar mustache-like design. Colorful cartonnage plaques lay on the bandages. Nearby, there's a small menagerie of mummified animals, including two cats, a tiny crocodile, and a hawk. Most of these animals are just little bundles that resemble well-worn stuffed toys rather than taxidermied trophies. In the same display case with Minister Cox and the little animals, a huge carved coffin stands above it all, and other Egyptian artifacts surround it. Further along the Western Cultures hall, a mummified bull takes up a large glass case of its own. The bull mummy actually looks more like a wrapped Jabba the Hutt with a bull's head attached, because the mummifier cheated a little. It turns out that the bandages contain only the loose bones of the animal, and the form is filled out to life-size with cloth stuffing. The bull's painted eyes are nice touches, though.

The Smithsonian supplements its mummy displays with a series of short films about mummies, tombs, and mummification ritual and practice that are shown simultaneously in two small amphitheaters. "Mummies Under Wraps" introduces three mummies: "Indiana Jones," "Ancient Annie," and "Minister Cox," who undergo the prying indignities of x-ray and CAT scans while still fully "dressed." Why go to such trouble to examine a mummy when a scissors would do? Well, it seems mummies may last thousands of years, but only if they aren't disturbed. They're actually very fragile. Using see-through technology helps anthropologists avoid damaging the mummy as they determine its gender, age, cause of death, and how long ago they lived.

Like the Smithsonian, Baltimore's Walters Gallery displays a fully wrapped mummy covered in its finely painted cartonnage. You can't see the actual mummy under the bandages, but you can examine the funerary symbols painted on the cartonnage, which include the four sons of Horus, male figures with jackal, falcon, baboon, and human heads. Because they help protect the deceased, the sons are also represented in the form of canopic jars, which are displayed with other ancient Egyptian artifacts. Now that the gallery's renovation is complete, their second mummy is also on display. If you have kids along, ask at the main desk for the Walters' Art Packs on "Myths and Monsters" and "Ancient Wonders" for background information, stories of beliefs and myths, and creative thought questions to help you understand the collection.

If the mummy at the Johns Hopkins University (JHU) Archaeological Collection were to come to life like in the movies, it wouldn't have been able to get out of its rock hard bandages. Mummifiers prepared this mummy by pouring pitch over the linen wrappings, which hardened to keep out moisture. To examine the mummy, scientists chiseled away the wrappings from the waist up, revealing a skeletal figure with blackened, leathery skin. It's eerie to see the figure's naked head, chest, and crossed arms—not to mention the fingernails and even the nerve endings poking out of the left arm! Later examinations by x-ray and CAT scans have given the mummy back some of its identity. We know this mummy was a female, aged 40 to 55 years old, and had a couple of children. More than that, we know she was a member of the upper class.

"She's very well mummified," says JHU Egyptologist Betsy Bryan. "That's probably the best indication of social status. The flank incision indicated a more careful process; it shows the organs were removed manually. She's in remarkable condition, too. She shows no arthritic problems despite her age, which also shows upper class status." The x-rays—which are displayed—reveal wrapped bundles in the mummy's chest cavity; according to subsequent CAT scans, these bundles contain her internal organs. JHU also has a cat mummy displayed with its own x-ray. And there's a burial mask and canopic jars among its teaching collection of everyday artifacts from Ancient Egypt and the Roman Empire.

Mummies weren't only made by the Ancient Egyptians, and they aren't always intentional. The first Egyptian mummies resulted when the Egyptians buried their dead in sand pits, and the sand dried out the bodies. As they developed tomb burials, the Egyptians discovered that the exposure to air was not good for preservation, so they developed their elaborate mummification techniques.

The Iceman is another example of natural mummification. He was freeze-dried by wind and dehydration while he was crossing the Alps 5,300 years ago. Snow and glacier ice protected his body from exposure and decay. Discovered in 1991, the Iceman is now preserved in a special refrigerated case at a museum in Italy. You can see photographs of his discovery in a small display, "Frozen in Time: The Iceman," at the Smithsonian's National Museum of Natural History, on the way to the Egyptian rooms.

In modern times, body parts have been preserved for medical study. The National Museum of Health and Medicine (see the article in this book) displays a number of well-preserved specimens showing cutaway views of muscle and bone to illustrate face and neck structure and reproductive systems. These lifelike and explicit displays are not for the squeamish or immature.

It may be a long drive to Phillipi, West Virginia, home of the "Mummies of the Insane," but the creepy shiver of horror at the end makes it worthwhile. This pair of female mummies was preserved in 1888 by a local man who acquired the bodies from the West Virginia Hospital for the Insane in order to test a Biblical mummification recipe. P.T. Barnum once took these mummies on a European tour, and now they reside at the Barbour County Historical Museum. These mummies were never wrapped, and a loincloth is the only thing that protects you from the sight of their naked skeletal bodies and leathery skin. The mummies may be gruesome, but the formula was apparently successful.

And since the scare's the same whether the mummy's real or fake, you might want to examine the mummy replicas at Baltimore's American Dime Museum, the home of sideshow curiosities. Made about ten years ago by artist Mark Frierson, the "Devil Man" has horns and cloven hoofs for feet. There's also a Peruvian Amazon mummy from the Nelson Supply Company, dating to the turn of the last century when mummies were so common that museums actually wanted sensational fakes to draw a crowd. A couple things will tell you this truly rare specimen is a fake. For one thing, it's nine feet long; for another, it's still in the original box with pressed leather trim. Then there are the "Australian sand mummies," anatomically correct replicas once used on the carnival midway. Fakes or not, these mummies aren't going anywhere, no matter what the horror movies tell you.

Mondo Mummy Guide

American Dime Museum, 1808 Maryland Ave., Baltimore, MD. (410) 230-0263. Website: www.dimemuseum.net. Hours W-F 12-3 p.m.; Sat & Sun 12-5 p.m. Cost: Adults $5; children ages 6-12 $3.

Barbour County Historical Museum, 146 N. Main St., Phillipi, WV. (304) 457-3349; for appointments call (304) 457-4846. Website: www. westsylvania.com/cfm/attractions_detail.cfm?asset_id=34887.   Hours: June 3-Oct M-Sat 11 a.m.-4 p.m.; Sun 1-4 p.m.; by appointment all other times. Cost $1.

The Johns Hopkins University Archaeological Collection, 129/130 Gilman Hall, 3400 N. Charles St., Baltimore, MD. (410) 516-7561. Website: www.jhu.edu/~archaeo/. Hours change by semester; call for times or appointment. Cost: Free.

National Museum of Health and Medicine, 6900 Georgia Avenue and Elder St., NW, AFIP, Building 54, (Walter Reed Army Medical Center), WDC. (202) 782-2200. Website: www.nmhm.washingtondc.museum/. Hours: 10 a.m.-5:30 p.m. daily. Cost: Free.

Smithsonian National Museum of Natural History, 10th and Constitution, WDC. (202) 633-1000. Website: www.mnh.si.edu/. Hours: Open daily 10 a.m. to 5:30 p.m. Cost: Free. You can find an overview of the ancient Egyptian mummification process at the Smithsonian's website: www.si.edu/resource/faq/nmnh/mummies.htm. The Iceman is featured at www.pbs.org/wgbh/nova/icemummies/.

Walters Art Museum, 600 N. Charles St., Baltimore, MD. (410) 547-9000. Website: www.thewalters.org. Hours: W-Sun 10 a.m.-5 p.m. Cost: Adults $8; seniors and ages 18-25 $5; ages 6-17 Free.

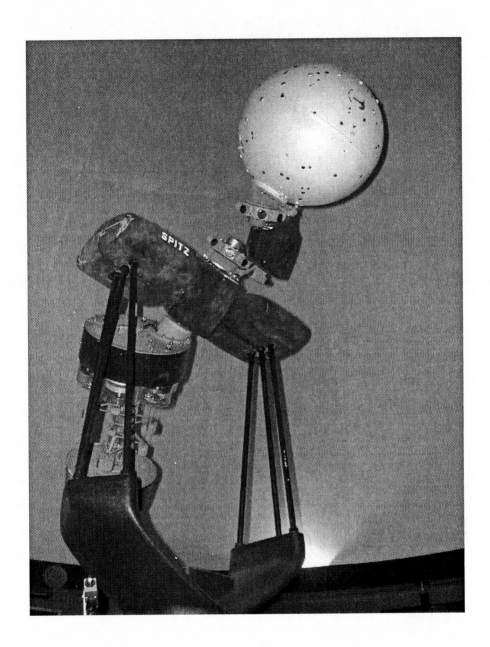

Mondo Planetarium: A Guide to the Planetariums in the DC Area

If you've ever enjoyed the beauty of the night sky but found the multitude of stars too chaotic to understand, a visit to one of the DC area's planetariums can help you make sense of it all. The first requirement for being an astronomer, it turns out, is a love of looking up at night.

"Astronomy is the oldest science and one of the few sciences that welcomes amateurs. Everyone who looks up in the stars with wonder is an astronomer," writes Harold Williams on the Montgomery College Planetarium's website. During his presentations, Williams, an adjunct professor at Montgomery College, in Takoma Park, Maryland, and the director of its planetarium, emphasizes the simplicity of basic skills that inform a do-it-yourself approach. "Once you understand the principles," he says, "you can figure things out for yourself—which is always better."

Rock Creek Park Ranger and Planetarium Director Ron Harvey agrees. The weekend matinees he produces are geared to kids and emphasize the basic astronomy tool everyone has access to. "I want to encourage people to get out there and look up," Harvey says. "Hopefully, one day we'll say we don't need the planetarium anymore. We can just go outside and look up. I want to give [visitors] a key to understanding what's up there. Nothing beats the real thing."

At a recent 4:00 p.m. showing of "Exploring the Universe," a group of seven year old boys enthusiastically celebrated a friend's birthday in Rock Creek's planetarium, oohing and ahhing as the thirty-two year old Spitz projector rotated the stars on the dome above their heads. Many of the boys seemed familiar with the Big Dipper as Harvey demonstrated techniques for using this basic stellar formation (or asterism) to identify the constellation to which it belongs, Ursa Major, or the Great Bear. Using two stars in the Big Dipper's bowl as a baseline, Harvey mapped out the North Star, the Summer Triangle, and the Northern Cross, which forms part of the constellation Cygnus, the Swan. He also talked about the planets, comets, meteors, and the Milky Way as part of a grand tour that unfolded overhead in slides and moving images overlaid on the basic star projection.

Williams' universe tour at Montgomery College is more in-depth. While Harvey mentions the plane of the ecliptic, the circle the sun and planets make as they appear to orbit the earth through the signs of the zodiac, Williams uses his newer Spitz model to project grids of the ecliptic and the meridian lines. After a viewing of the constellations and other celestial phenomena, Williams turns to a discussion of a specific topic, rotating these throughout the year.

As the crowd of visitors left the Montgomery College Planetarium after a recent show, we found that the moon and Mars had risen over the trees directly in front of us. Suddenly, the sky seemed so simple. The ability of the planetarium to create a map of the sky using overlaid graphs and diagrams, and to show stellar formations and movements over time, really makes that confusing placement of celestial objects seem logical for once.

After his shows, Williams sets up a telescope in the planetarium parking lot to give visitors a closer look at these objects. The Rock Creek Nature Center, in Washington, DC, also offers monthly telescope viewings in a program called "Exploring the Sky," with topics varying by season. Most planetariums follow their multimedia shows with hands-on telescope viewings, when weather permits.

Clouds and rainy weather aren't the only obstacles to clear viewing; the glare of light pollution is a more serious problem. Every planetarium guide laments the detrimental effect of city lights on our ability to enjoy and study the full star field. Ironically, the lights we use to get around in the darkness erode a natural resource that our ancestors depended on as a navigational tool. As an astronomer at the only National Park with a planetarium, Harvey particularly notes that the starry night sky "is a resource that's not just in the park. That's one of the things we [rangers] have to take care of. That's why we have legislation against light pollution."

Despite the lower visibility in our urban environment, Candice Wilson, coordinator of the Arlington Planetarium, in Virginia, is encouraging: "You can see the major asterisms through light pollution, things like the Big Dipper, the Summer Triangle, Orion, and Cassiopeia. We're so far removed from the dark skies that we wouldn't be able to identify everything [anyway]. We'd be overwhelmed."

While planetariums pack enough educational fun for the H. B. Owens Science Center's website to call them the "theme parks of the universe," Wilson considers the planetarium a guide to the more spiritual benefits of astronomy available to everyone, as well. "If people weren't so intimidated by the stars, they'd find comfort in them," she says. "The stars give people a bigger perspective. They instill wonder in people's psyches; they can lead people to diversion and comfort and peace."

Mondo Planetarium Guide

It's best to call or check websites for information on scheduled programs, as these vary with the season.

Albert Einstein Planetarium, National Air and Space Museum, Sixth St. and Independence Ave., SW, WDC. (202) 357-1686, or (202) 357-2700. Website: http://www.nasm.si.edu/visit/planetarium/. Open daily 10 a.m. to 5:30 p.m. "The Stars Tonight," a 30-minute lecture on the current night sky, is presented daily at noon. "Infinity Express" a "20-minute tour of the universe," repeats throughout the day starting at 10:30 a.m. Cost for these presentations is $5.50 per person; a reduced price "combo ticket" package is also available.

Arlington Planetarium, 1426 N. Quincy St., Arlington, VA. (703) 228-6070. Website: www.arlington.k12.va.us/instruct/science/planetarium. Multimedia shows weekly on Fridays and Saturdays at 7:30 p.m., plus Sunday matinees at 1:30 p.m. and 3 p.m. "The Stars Tonight," a lecture on the current night sky, runs the first Monday of each month from September through June at 7:30 p.m. Admission is $2.50 for adults; $1.50 for children and seniors.

Howard B. Owens Science Center, 9601 Greenbelt Rd., Lanham, MD. (301) 918-8750. Website: www.pgcps.org/~hbowens/planetarium. html. Planetarium shows on the second Friday of each month from October to June at 7:30 p.m. Check website for program information. Cost is $4 for adults; $2 for students, kids under 12 and seniors.

Montgomery College Planetarium, Takoma Ave. and Fenton St., Takoma Park, MD. (301) 650-1463. Website: www.mc.cc.md.us/Departments/planet/. Monthly public planetarium programs at 7 p.m. running from September through May. Check website for program information. Free.

Rock Creek Park Planetarium, Rock Creek Nature Center, 5200 Glover Rd., NW, WDC. (202) 895-6070. Website: www.nps.gov/rocr/planetarium/. Planetarium shows are offered Saturdays and Sundays. "The Night Sky," at 1 p.m., focuses on the current star map, identifying major constellations and the movement of the heavenly bodies through the night sky. (Children under four are not admitted.) Advanced planetarium shows at 4 p.m. feature more in-depth topics and change weekly; call or check website for schedule. (Children under seven are not admitted.) An evening program called "Exploring the Sky" offers hands-on telescope viewing of the real night sky; these sessions are held once a month on Saturdays from April through November (check website for times and program information). The majority of these programs show the night sky as it appears in the DC area for the specific date and time of the program. Free tickets can be picked up at the information desk in the Nature Center.

Mr. Dixie: Suburban Cowboy

111 Gordon Rd.
Falls Church, VA
(703) 533-1111
Viewing hours: Anytime
Cost: Free

At eleven feet tall, Mr. Dixie may be the biggest Southern gentleman in the DC area. He'd love for y'all to drop by anytime, day or night—he's on 24-7 guard duty for the Dixie Sheet Metal Works, in Falls Church, Virginia. The shop's just down Gordon Road from former Virginia Lieutenant Governor Don Beyer's car dealership. (Beyer's empire is a sight in itself. The offices are disguised as a Norman Rockwell-style small town, and a cast-iron statue of a farmer slopping his hogs stands at the street corner in front of the showroom.) I've never bought any sheet metal, but Mr. Dixie is very helpful in pointing the way past the Dixie sales office toward the Falls Church recycling center.

A black cowboy hat on his turbovane head and his stovepipe-duct legs bowed, Mr. Dixie looks like he just dismounted from his horse. His huge belt buckle is a supply register from an air conditioning unit, and red reflectors serve as buttons on his classic red shirt. His chest, arms, legs, and hat are made from hand-cut pieces of sheet metal, constructed according to the owners' plans back in 1962.

"The idea was to use a turbine for a head and make the rest of the body proportional to that," remembers Dixie co-owner Larry Degast, who's now retired.

"The guy who made him was just out of school, had real talent," says Bobby Withers, another shop co-owner. "You can't hire somebody to make something like that now. All the cutting is done by computer. Used to be if you could draw it on a piece of paper, they could make it. We have people who can do that here, but we couldn't hire anybody new."

"It was Butch Kilpatrick that made him," co-owner Paul Puckett declares on a recent visit. Has anybody at the shop made anything else like Mr. Dixie? "No, that takes a sculptural interest," Puckett says. "We help sculptors make things, though."

Mr. Dixie debuted on a Falls Church Memorial Day parade float the same year he was made. The original float version touched his hat and was identical on each side; that way, he could greet people both coming and going as he passed on his pickup bed perch. "The idea was he was a

Southern gentleman," Degast recalls, adding, "We had four young ladies on the back throwing out candy kisses and such."

After the parade, Mr. Dixie's arms were repositioned and he was placed on top of the office building on the corner of Gordon Road and Broad Street, pointing out the sheet metal shop's office on Gordon Road. When the top floor was rented to Hazelton Labs, it was discovered that Mr. Dixie's turbovane head squeaked as it turned in the wind—and the noise badly agitated the lab's experimental monkeys. At the researchers' request, the tin man was removed. Hazelton Labs later moved to the Reston, Virginia, area, where a snafu with a viral outbreak became the inspiration for the *Hotzone* book and the movie *Outbreak*, starring Dustin Hoffman.

Another retired shop co-owner, Hap Atkinson, remembers Mr. Dixie's move was prompted by a City of Falls Church sign ordinance. Whether the result of nascent PETA activism or law-abiding citizenship, Mr. Dixie was posted at his present location in the late-1960s. Here, the tin man has enjoyed the passing decades free of vandalism, fending off only friendly purchase bids. There are patches where the paint is flaking off, but he's in great condition otherwise. His only misadventure was a prank orchestrated by the shop's staff in which Mr. Dixie gained a male appendage fashioned from a cardboard tube. "He was a proud tin man for a while," Withers remarks, gleefully recalling the incident.

Just how much is the tin man worth? "We wouldn't sell him," Puckett declares. "If we closed the place, we'd just give him away."

"He's just a good conversation piece," Withers adds.

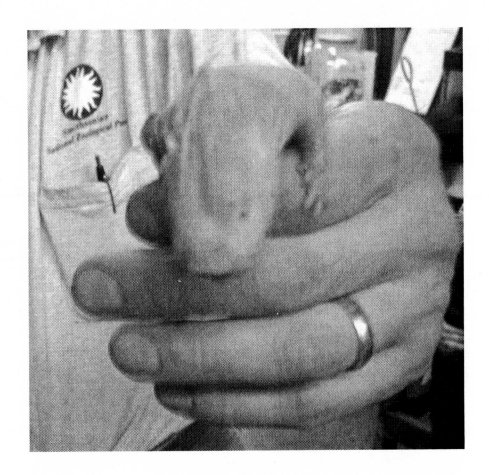

Naked Mole-Rat Tunnels

Small Mammal House, National Zoo
3001 Connecticut Ave, NW
Washington, DC
(202) 673-4800
Website: www.nationalzoo.si.edu/Animals/SmallMammals
www.nationalzoo.si.edu/support/adoptspecies/animalinfo/
nakedmolerat/default.cfm
Hours: 8 a.m.-8 p.m. daily
Cost: Free

Quick, name the world's weirdest land animal. How about the hyrax—which looks like a groundhog but is related to the elephant? Surely the duckbilled platypus? Or the echidna, an egg layer also known as the spiny anteater?

Nope. All of these creatures have a little bit too much in common with us *homo sapiens*. So what beastie could be weirder? Would you believe a mammal that's cold blooded like a reptile, lives like social insects with a single queen, requires low levels of oxygen, and resembles, uh, how about a fetal sausage with buck teeth? For sheer oddness, you just can't beat the naked mole-rat (known to biologists as *Heterocephalus glaber*).

You can get a good look at these tiny critters in their special see-through tunnels at the National Zoo's Small Mammal House. And then you just might look away in horror, disgust, or embarrassment. These tubular, hairless things have wrinkled pink skins and a single pair of huge protruding teeth. "They've been described as 'a sausage stuffed with walnuts,' or 'saber tooth hot dogs,'" notes their chief caretaker David S. Kessler, a Biologist at the Small Mammal House. "And there's a few obscene descriptions," he adds. Like, a penis with teeth, maybe? Appearance alone may explain why the naked mole-rats leave procreation to professionals—their queen and her two or three consorts, that is.

But seriously...no one currently knows why most naked mole-rats—that would be the workers and soldiers—completely forego reproductive behaviors. When it comes to these animals, there are more questions than answers, and even the answers are mysterious. Scientists currently have two hypotheses for how the queen suppresses the sex drive of her subordinates. The first involves pheromones that each mole-rat picks up when they roll in their urine and feces...

Gee, another mystery already! I told you these critters were weird! At least this behavior can be explained. Mole-rats are blind and rely on scent to identify their den mates. But there could be a pheromone in the queen's urine that causes sexual repression, although Kessler points out that research has pretty much eliminated this hypothesis.

The second theory involves physical intimidation. "The queen really pushes a lot of the other colony members around," Kessler says rapidly, clearly relishing every quirk of his little charges. "And it's thought that by [doing this] that she somehow suppresses the sexuality of the other animals."

So we're getting the big picture of mole-rat life here. One queen equals one mother, who's also a despotic ruler to rival any human dictator. There are usually two or three consorts, which the queen chooses from among the soldier class. That means everyone in the colony is very closely related—inbred, in fact! (OK, so there are more and more very good reasons for the asexuality of the naked mole-rat.) Genetically, mole-rats are so similar they're practically clones. The scientists who study them hypothesize that workers and soldiers don't mind that they don't have offspring of their own because their genes are being passed on anyway.

And the weirdness continues. Naked mole-rats live 10 to 30 years, a remarkable longevity compared to other small animals! They communicate with each other using at least eighteen different vocalizations! And the queen produces four litters of twenty pups per year, a bigger litter size than any other mammal!

Naked mole-rat fandom doesn't rest in reciting obscure details of their metabolism, eusocial behavior (that's "hive lifestyle" to you and me), or reproductive quirks. No, ladies and gentlemen, a visit to the naked mole-rat tunnels is an unparalleled theatrical entertainment! When two mole-rats meet in their transparent tunnels, they begin playing a kind of existential leapfrog, where one animal will climb over the other, and then the second will climb over the first...again and again and again. Quite often, they'll nudge a chunk of food ever so slightly as they flip flop in place. Samuel Beckett himself couldn't have penned a more pointless drama.

"I think of it as just jockeying for position," Kessler says firmly. "People say they're fighting, but no, they're not fighting—when they fight, they kill. It's more like a little sibling rivalry. Also, in the wild when they dig their tunnels, they set up these little bucket brigades without the buckets. There's a whole bunch of mole-rats, and one will dig and kick the dirt back, and it will keep getting kicked back...Normally what would happen is the front one would get tired from digging, and another one would come and take its place. Now the one in the back is taking the place, but the front one is still willing to work. So it's not necessarily pointless for them."

When Kessler first saw them doing this absurd dance, he was concerned. Oftentimes, an odd repetitive behavior by a caged animal is a sign of stress. But after careful examination, he decided they were acting normally, at least given the limited knowledge of mole-rat activity. "I'm pretty sure it's not a neurotic artifact of captivity, that it is a natural behavior, but one of the stopping points for that behavior is not there," Kessler explains. "What's interesting is that it's not shirking the work behavior. It's more kind of jockeying to be the worker." But despite more than a decade in their company, he's just as mystified as the rest of us. "You know, I don't ascribe any motivations," he jokes. "I can't get into their tiny little naked mole-rat brains."

Kessler's been trying to figure these guys out since 1991, when the National Zoo acquired twenty naked mole-rats from the Philadelphia Zoo. He's shepherded that original group through 300 successful births and multiple colony splittings. The National Zoo has given naked mole-rats to many other zoos, and currently has three colonies of them, two of which are in a separate research facility. Kessler also initiated the "naked mole-rat cam" project, the first webcam for the zoo's website. Just log on to www. nationalzoo.si.edu/Animals/SmallMammals for a little preview of mole-rat life—usually a pile of sleeping sausages. Kessler quickly adds that the camera is not focused on the exhibited animals, but on one of the research center's colonies.

When you visit, you'll notice that the zoo also has two other colonies on exhibit, each containing a different species of mole-rat—but both have fur. The Damaraland mole-rat is a distant relation to the naked mole-rat, but the Middle East blind mole-rat is a much more distant cousin. In the exhibit area, the Damaraland mole-rats' tunnels are above the naked mole-rat tunnels. The Middle East mole-rat lives alone in a small set of tunnels toward the back; a sign near his home calls him a Palestine mole-rat, the name his species was once known by. Both Damaraland and Middle East mole-rats more closely resemble familiar small mammals, like moles and hamsters. So they're not quite so alien to the rest of us in the mammal kingdom.

Kessler is also responsible for choosing the Habitrail-style look of the zoo's mole-rat display over the naturalistic design employed by most other zoos. "I purposely designed the exhibit to look unnatural, and that's for several reasons," Kessler says excitedly. He's on another roll. "One is when you see a naturalistic looking exhibit, if it's got gunnite trees and concrete rocks, it's not really natural for the animals, it's naturalistic for the people looking at it. Naked mole-rats are blind!" he snaps. "So I wanted an exhibit that felt natural to them, and smelled natural, and seemed natural to them, but may not look natural to the visitors. I wanted there to be an implicit message that you could be natural without looking natural."

The clear tube that goes out into the public area was another of Kessler's design innovations. "When I picked up the original colony, my son at the time was six, and he was looking at them from underneath. I wanted something so kids could get nose to nose with mole-rats—and so the animals could get away from the kids if they wanted to."

As mole-rats naturally live in complete darkness, does the light of the exhibit area bother them?

The short answer is that being blind, mole-rats may not be terribly sensitive to light, any more than they're bothered by people standing nearby. A bigger problem is their incredibly sensitive hearing. "They're very sensitive to sound, and if they're all freaked out because of the noise of people coming around, they're not going to be good exhibit animals, and it's gonna stress them out," Kessler notes with concern. "We don't want to stress out our animals. So before we put them on exhibit we acclimate them to light and sound. We have a radio going all the time, and that gets them used to the sounds. It doesn't seem to affect them in terms of their longevity, their health, or their reproductive success. Those are the criteria we use to judge if an animal is being stressed."

And it doesn't affect their appetite, either. The zoo's naked mole-rats chow down on sweet potatoes, carrots, turnips, kale, celery, apples, and corn, plus a "leaf eater biscuit" that's "good for their teeth," Kessler assures me. "It's something we feed to a lot of our animals, from rodents to primates." A few years ago, the mole-rats also got a special food the zoo's nutritionists cooked up; called "naked mole-rat goo," the stuff looked like gelatin and combined vegetable puree with some ground-up rodent blocks and other nutritional supplements. "The mole-rats eventually stopped eating it." Kessler doesn't sound surprised. "If animals will eat a good, balanced natural diet, that's what we want to keep them on."

In the wild, mole-rats mostly feed on giant tubers that can grow up to 100 pounds, eating the inside of the tuber and leaving a living shell that the plant can continue to grow and use as a food source. "I am told that [the tubers] taste closest to a jicama," Kessler notes. "You often get it in some Mexican food; it's very tasty." They're also known to harvest some greens by pulling them down into their tunnels from below ground, he says: "They're like little cartoon animals that pull the plants down."

Naked mole-rats are native only to the Horn of Africa—that is, Somalia, Kenya, and Ethiopia—where they're called "sand puppies." The first Westerner described them in a scientific paper in 1848, and in the early 1950s the London Zoological Society studied two mole-rats for eleven days before the animals died. It was the 1970s before scientists understood that they were organized in a hive society. Kessler remarks, "Some animals you can keep in captivity without understanding their social structure. Not so with naked mole-rats." These animals simply cannot survive without their den mates.

So scientists and zookeepers must have a heck of a time bringing them to the United States. Kessler can't comment on that, as all his mole-rats have come from the same Philadelphia colony. But he understands their special requirements, having transported small colonies to other zoos. For short trips, he loads the animals into Coleman coolers, the ideal solution for cold-blooded animals that must be kept warm, yet don't need much oxygen. This doesn't work so well for long-distance trips, simply because the mole-rats can chew their way out. When Kessler shipped some of the animals to Seattle once, the shop crew built a stainless steel container to fit inside the cooler. If they used a softer metal, the mole-rats would chew through it.

"Our shop guy constructed a little grate for me once," Kessler recalls, "because I wanted to divide part of the colony, but I wanted them to be in contact with one another. It was a little grate with holes in it, and it was made out of aluminum. They ate through that in forty-five minutes."

The naked mole-rats meet few substances strong enough to hold them back. "Twenty-five percent of their musculature is around their jaw. It's as if you took all the muscles from one of your legs and moved it around your mouth," Kessler says with awe. "So forget hyenas and tigers and lions," he adds with the gleeful pride of the small-mammal scientist who's got a topper on the kings of the animal kingdom, "when you want to talk about the most muscle mass for body size, it's the naked mole-rat. They can chew through concrete; they can bite through a human hand—I've seen 'em do both! They're pretty impressive."

Kessler pauses for effect. "On the other hand, their teeth are so sensitive, they'll pick up the pups, which weigh only a gram and are very thin skinned, and you will not see a mark on the pup after they've been picked up. And when they sleep, sometimes you can see this if you watch the webcam, they will bruxillate—they'll grind their teeth when they're sleeping. They're sharpening and honing their teeth." On top of that, the added muscles and nerves around their teeth give the mole-rats such control they can move them like chopsticks to pick things up!

Does all this mean the naked mole-rats have the ultimate escape plan at the ready? Not really—because they can't get a grip on the rounded tunnels. "If you use square chambers," Kessler declares, "they'll find a little corner and dig through that!"

National Bonsai and Penjing Museum

U.S. National Arboretum
3501 New York Ave, NE
Washington, DC
(202) 245-4575
Website: www.bonsai-nbf.org
Hours: 10 a.m.-3:30 p.m. daily
Cost: Free

There's something special about rocks. They're fun to pick up, throw, collect, examine. But what do you do when you find a rock that seems to glare back at you, threatening to haunt you for the rest of your days? Fortunately, the person who found just such a rock in the Lingbi County of China's Anhui province hauled it home and eventually donated it to the "viewing stone" collection at the National Bonsai and Penjing Museum. The most startling of the viewing stones here, the "Lingbi Rock" resembles petrified smoke, or a hooded, spectral figure lurking in the background of a Dali-painted desert landscape. Watch it long enough and you can almost see it curling up into the air, hunching over to examine you more closely. You're supposed to meditate on these stones, but with this one, you may not be able to tear your eyes away for fear it will follow you!

Leave it to the Chinese to develop stone appreciation into an art form. Called "gongshi," or "scholar's rocks," the point of this ancient art is to pick special stones that possess "a character that leads the viewer...to imagine a scene of undisturbed grandeur and to enter a poetic world of solitude and tranquility" (as the collection's catalog, *Awakening the Soul*, puts it). While the scholars in China preferred vertical rocks in abstract shapes, the Japanese developed "suiseki" to focus on horizontally oriented stones that resemble natural scenes; the Koreans had a similar goal for their art of "suseok." Stones from all three nations and North America comprise the viewing stone collection, housed in the museum's Mary Mrose International Pavilion. It's the largest collection of viewing stones on public display in America.

Most viewing stones look like natural scenes—there's lots of mountain vistas and plateaus on display here. One strange blob has a patch of white that seems very much like a frothy spring bubbling from the center of the rock. Someone called it the "Waterfall Stone," and it's just as cool, refreshing, and relaxing as watching the real thing. More unusual are the chrysanthemum stones from Japan, which look like flowers blooming inside the rock. These squarish chunks are actually embedded with crystal formations that resemble chrysanthemum flowers, a traditional Asian symbol of immortality. The museum's "Moon Night Chrysanthemum Stone" is said to be one of the finest of its kind in the world.

Aside from the Lingbi, the wildest of all the stones are two other examples from China. The "Mountain Lake Stone" and "Taihu Rock" resemble the skulls of a Dr. Seuss beast with dozens of eye sockets and several fused jaws set in a long, twisted head. On a recent visit, these two limestone rocks were displayed in the model Chinese scholar's studio, in an alcove by the International Pavilion's entrance.

"They're hard to come by in those unique shapes," the museum's Supervisory Curator Jack Sustic confirms. "The one that's in the scholar's studio, the Taihu Rock, the holes in that are generally created by man. Sometimes they create those and put them back in the water. That softens them for further erosion." Lingbi rocks, however, are excavated from deep mud, and are naturally shaped. That mysterious, smoke-like stone in the museum's collection is cantilevered so perfectly that it is not affixed to its base, but rests there naturally. The museum has about a hundred viewing stones in its collection, so they are rotated in special displays about every month, allowing for a good sampling of pieces on each visit.

Obviously, viewing stones are only a small part of the National Bonsai and Penjing Museum; mostly, it's a unique repository of those shrunken poodle trees that provoke amusement in some and awe in others. If it's possible for a place to be too peaceful, this museum would be that place. A stroll through the collection spread out over three open air pavilions and one greenhouse offers over 150 opportunities for meditation! Each tree tells fascinating stories of the human gardeners and forces of nature that worked for decades to shape the living work of art before you. When you consider that a single tree may outlive several caretakers, who must pick up the careful shaping and pruning to fulfill a design started decades before, the museum is also something of a monument to patience—but in a good way. It's easy to find pleasure contemplating these examples of essential tree-ness.

Or forest-ness, as the case may be. A breathtaking example of the bonsai art, an arrangement of foemina juniper called "Goshin" (meaning "protector of the spirit") looks like an old growth redwood forest seen from a vast distance. Spires of dead white trunk tower over spreading branches of green foliage, vividly reminding us that these are living things. "That's probably the most famous bonsai in the world," Sustic notes. "Definitely the most famous in the United States. It was created by the father of American bonsai, John Nakai. There are eleven trees in that forest, and he has eleven grandchildren. So that's one example of a story that makes us appreciate the trees more."

The oldest bonsai is a 380 year old (and counting) Japanese White Pine, measuring a rather gargantuan three feet tall. With its fat, stubby trunk and wide canopy, with each needle obediently pointing upward, it vaguely resembles a funky scrub brush. This tree, Sustic tells me, was in one family in Japan for six generations!

One of the most striking trees, a California Juniper, has a dramatically arching trunk of white deadwood bowed so deeply that the new growth actually starts below the pot. Closer inspection shows that growth follows a line of living tissue leading back to the roots. The tree seems to be offering its carefully balanced canopy for you to study the way it uses light and space and form.

This specimen was collected and designed by Mr. California Juniper, aka bonsai master Harry Hirao. Like most bonsai, the sweeping juniper is the result of the epic struggle between time, human effort, and nature. The California Juniper "tend to naturally grow in kind of a slump," Sustic explains. "The center will die out, and it will slowly grow and send out these shoots. You can dig up a California Juniper clump, and depending on the size of it, you could get four or five trees out of it, just by the nature of the way it grows. There are others in a different location that may just be one specimen." Still, Hirao must have been astonished when he found this tree during a routine collecting excursion at a large farm, as it had been holding its shape for some time. Sustic continues, "The general rule is that for every inch of bark it's about seventy-five years old. So we figure that tree is well over 1,000 years old. It definitely hasn't been a bonsai that long."

So what does the bonsai artist do, in this case? Where does the art come in? Part of any gardener's effort is just keeping the plant alive, but in bonsai, there's an aesthetic appearance that also must be maintained. "If you look you'll see the live part of the tree, the cambium," Sustic points out, explaining the caretaker's challenge. "The Japanese call it the water line; we often call it the life line. [The tree will live] as long as it has that, and [the cambium] can be relatively small. Depending on the amount of foliage it has to support, it could be the size of a pencil. In this tree's case, it's about the size of your forearm, or your wrist in any case. We treat the deadwood with a wood preservative, and that keeps it from rotting. If we didn't do anything to [the wood], it would eventually disappear, like in nature."

The marvels continue in rows: tree after tree set on rough wooden tables lining the perimeter of each building, arranged like sculptures against stark white walls—all the better to examine their shapes. The pavilions are dedicated to three different schools of bonsai. First is the Chinese, where the art began under the name "penjing," then Japanese, and finally North American, with architecture to match each culture. The Chinese Pavilion is most recognizably marked by a giant scholar's rock outside a gate with a traditional Chinese style roof. The fourth pavilion is a greenhouse reserved for tropical plants, like banyan, buttonwood, and Fukien tea. One gorgeous tea tree echoes the sweeping juniper in the American Pavilion. The large deadwood arch on this tree, Sustic says, is the result of a vascular disease. "Instead of cutting it off, we thought it would be interesting to try to keep it," he explains. These two trees are fine examples of the "cascade style" of bonsai.

You'll find the Bonsai Museum fairly easily on the sprawling grounds of the National Arboretum, just behind the Visitor's Center—and across the patio from the koi pond that surrounds it like a moat. After you've let those giant goldfish gulp food pellets right from your fingers, you're ready to get serious about peace and quiet. The gongshi and bonsai await.

National Capital Trolley Museum

1313 Bonifant Road
Colesville, MD
(301) 384-6088
Website: www.dctrolley.org
Hours: Jan 2-Nov 30: Sat & Sun 12-5 p.m.;
March 15-May 15: additional Th & F 10 a.m.-2 p.m.
June 15-Aug 15: additional Th & F 11 a.m.-3 p.m.
Oct 1-Nov 15: additional Th & F 10 a.m.-2 .m.
Cost: Free admission; trolley ride fares—adults: $3; children
and seniors: $2

The Washington area lost its trolley privileges for the second time on September 28, 2003. That night at 2 a.m., a devastating blaze started in one of the garages housing part of the National Capital Trolley Museum's collection of priceless antique street cars. As firemen fought the flames for an hour, eight trolleys melted into scrap. Among the losses were two irreplaceable passenger trolleys that once served DC's streets: an 1899 "work car" called "0509" used into the 1930s, and a 1935 "Streamliner" called "1053." They also lost two work cars with large bamboo bristle brushes used to sweep snow from the DC tracks, three cars from Austria, and one from Johnstown, Pennsylvania. In all, the damage was estimated at $8-10 million dollars.

"This was more like a death," says Wesley Paulson, a museum volunteer since 1970. "Because there were friendships centered around the work on the cars, and a lot of memories of them with the equipment. And with it gone, we've kind of lost that attachment to people we worked with over the years."

During his time at the museum, Paulson has helped collect, maintain, and run the cars, and he currently wears the hat of Director of Development. But he's never seen anything like the aftermath of the fire.

"It was very devastating," Paulson recalls, his voice betraying emotion still strong after nearly a year. The Johnstown street car had just been overhauled to the tune of $100,000, not counting volunteer labor. DC's Streamliner was "one of a kind," he notes. "That was a developmental car, experimental for its time. It was one of ten built, and it was the last. For the real purist people who study things, it was the bridge between the old style street car, like the Johnstown car, and the more modern car of the 1940s and 1950s that's still used in San Francisco and other places." He still can't believe the loss. "Those two gave everybody a low blow."

The cause of the fire remains something of a mystery. The Fire Marshall's investigation ruled out arson or lightning, placing the blame instead on an overheated braking system in one of the trolleys driven that day. Paulson explains, "The official ruling was that it was 'accidental of unknown origin.' Something electrically hot that smoldered and found a source of oxygen and then went boom. The other part of the assumption is that it was burning for quite a while before it burned the roof off of the building. It wasn't until the roof burned off that anybody saw anything. It's like the building worked like a big oven and contained the fire. That created a high amount of heat and caused everything to melt."

The fire didn't keep the Trolley Museum down for long. They were back in business by October 11, reopening the exhibit house and showing visitors the fire damage. Relying on the surviving eleven street cars that were stored in another barn, the trolley rides resumed on October 30, just a month after the fire. The museum still owns two working passenger cars once used on the DC rails, plus three others stored off-site, which, admittedly, need a little work. The surviving cars of the "International Street Car Collection" include models from Berlin, Dusseldorf, The Hague, and Toronto. It also owns a car once used in New York City.

The original death knell for the DC street car had been rung in the late 1950s, when the first diesel buses began replacing the rail cars that had clanged the streets for more than half a century. All that's left today are a few stretches of rail visible on streets in Georgetown and other parts of the city.

But as the fire recovery has shown, the trolleys have dedicated friends. A group of transportation workers and trolley aficionados formally began collecting cars for the National Capital Trolley Museum in the late 1940s. After the museum was founded in 1959, the volunteers started building the railway loop and the first trolley barn (the one that burned). Fundraising paid for the other buildings, but maintenance chores—even roofing—are usually handled by the all-volunteer staff.

Other Washington area residents still had to wait until 1969 for a nostalgic trolley fix, when the museum opened to the public and began offering rides around a one mile loop of track set in the woods of Northwest Branch Park, in Montgomery County, Maryland. The volunteers make the experience complete by dressing in conductor uniforms and selling fare tickets, punching each one as you board.

On a recent visit, my son and I find ourselves riding the "4603," a 1950s era car once in service in Toronto. The trolley sways gently like a ship on rails, creaking and groaning through the woods. Trees surround us as the route partly follows the Northwest Branch of the Anacostia River, which we spot down the hill from the tracks. In roughly half an hour, we're back at the station, talking to our driver, Wells Drumwright.

Is the streetcar difficult to operate? I ask. "It's easy as pie," Drumwright tells me. "We're not streetcar professionals," he admits. "None of us have operated a streetcar anywhere but here."

Drumwright is a fountain of information about the cars, telling us that the "4603" we just rode is the largest car in the collection, at forty-six feet long. It weighs nineteen tons, and has four fifty-five horsepower motors— one on each axle. This particular car was refurbished while still owned by the Toronto Transit Commission; the museum acquired it in 1996. "The only thing original is the shell," Drumwright says. "It was updated in 1984 to an electrical system."

He's also full of wisdom about the streetcars. "We like the streetcar first of all because it doesn't pollute the air," he says with a grin. "Second, the ride is quieter than a bus. And it doesn't smell bad."

It may seem a little silly to drive out to the Maryland suburbs to ride public transportation, but sometimes you need to get away to a time that was slower, calmer, and more efficient. The trolleys run a road to nowhere—there's no other way to put it, really—but the view is beautiful, and the short cruise is a fun way to experience history. It's also a little sad finding out how comfortable—and comforting—a trolley's rocking gait can be. More than a jaunt through the woods on a life-sized model railroad, the trolley carries you back into the first half of the twentieth century. You could be in 1912, 1935, 1943, or 1950, depending on the car you're riding.

"It's a tangible link to a different time," Paulson says of the trolley attraction. "People often come out and recall not so much the car, but where they went, whether it was to the amusement park, or to the movies downtown. People who grew up in the 50s in Washington tend to say, 'I rode to school across town,' or 'I rode to Glen Echo.' [Seeing the trolleys provides] that linkage between now and then."

Come for the ride, then stick around to explore the background provided by the small exhibit area in the visitor's center. Here, you'll find a working model of the Chevy Chase Loop street car line, an interactive computer display showing the old DC trolley sites, plus those from Pittsburgh, San Francisco, and Toronto; model trolleys and a few toys, like the tin replica of the streetcar from the 1930s comic strip "Toonerville Trolley"; a film on trolley history; and displays of photos from DC's trolley-rich glory days.

And the next time you see rails in the street back in town, pause for a moment and close your eyes. You can just about hear that old trolley bell ring.

National Cryptologic Museum

National Security Agency
Colony 7 Rd.
Ft. George Meade, MD
(301) 688-5849
Website: www.nsa.gov/museum/index.cfm
Hours: M-F 9 a.m.-4 p.m., Sat 10 a.m.-2 p.m.
Cost: Free

To look at Mata Hari and James Bond, spying seems a glamorous business. But the real work of intelligence gathering lies in the tedium of cryptology and cryptanalysis, or code-making and -breaking, often best performed by mathematicians sitting at a desk. But don't let that deter you from stepping up to an amusing tour of the National Cryptologic Museum, which highlights the key personalities, coding and decoding machines, and wartime history of the field. There's playboy Secret Service man Herbert Yardley, the German Enigma machine (basically a hopped-up encoder ring), and the Bombe, a huge decoding device that preceded computers. From medieval textbooks to Native American code talkers to supercomputers and biometrics, the museum reveals that encryption technologies means excitement.

The museum actually had two grand openings. The first, on July 13, 1993, was only for National Security Agency (NSA) employees and their families, and the second, on December 17, 1993, introduced it to the public. But it had taken the NSA a while to decide that they even wanted a public museum that could tell the story of the agency and its accomplishments. From the time the NSA formed in 1952, it gained custody of the Army's Research and Development Museum Collection, a stash of obsolete cryptological artifacts from the previous decades. "In World War II and after, the services were collecting this stuff," Museum Curator Jack Ingram says, "and the NSA got it in 1952 when it formed. If it wasn't here, it would just take up room in government warehouses."

From the late 1970s through the 1980s, the NSA's history department maintained the collection, mounting small in-house displays to teach cryptological history to employees. Some pieces of equipment were loaned to the Smithsonian and other museums. When the Center for Cryptologic History was founded at the agency in 1989, its director, David W. Gaddy, pushed for a museum to house the growing collection of artifacts. Nonetheless, the ball didn't get rolling until the NSA bought the building adjacent to its offices: the Colony 7 Motel. After a little bureaucratic paper shuffling, the motel was granted to the museum, and from 1991 to April 1993, renovations began to turn the motel's office, restaurant, and dinner theater building into an exhibit hall. It's a remarkable recycling effort, even though the museum still looks like, well, an old motel. (Not that there's anything wrong with that!) Meanwhile, curator Jerry Coates and his assistant Jack Ingram were working to turn piles of old equipment into informative exhibits. The Smithsonian Museum of African Art made their job a little easier when it gave them a supply of display cases it was discarding. After the first opening, Coates and Ingram used employee feedback to polish displays and tour patter.

The museum isn't just a historical repository and educational resource; it also acts as an informal ambassador for the NSA. According to Ingram, who took over the curator's job after Coates retired, NSA employees especially like the museum. "They can bring their families," he explains. "This is as close as they can get them to what they do. And it shows them the history of what they do." That goes for the rest of us. Often called "No Such Agency," the NSA maintains strict secrecy of its operations in order to protect its latest encryption know-how.

Indeed, much of the loot on display was once highly classified. One of the most popular exhibits details the history and mechanics of the German Enigma machines used by the Nazis to encode their military intelligence. "If people have heard of anything, it's the Enigma," Ingram notes. "We rewrote the history of World War II when that information was declassified in the 70s." The Enigma doesn't look quite so important now, resembling a manual typewriter with dials. Key in a message and the dials electrically change the letters that come out. A half dozen different models squat mutely in glass cases, some exploded to show their inner workings. If it's a little tough to wrap your head around this stuff, the hands-on model can help you understand how the codes are produced. Well, it's fun to play with, anyway, especially as you're not likely to finger one at any other museums!

The Enigma produced codes that were so difficult to crack that the U.S. Navy had to develop a giant puzzle-solving machine—basically an analog precursor to the computer called "The Bombe"—to decipher them. Back in the day, 121 of these babies cost six million bucks to make; today, it's outdated junk taking up a lot of floor space. OK, it happens to the best of us. That's history for you!

If misery loves company, then so does obsolescence. The Bombe isn't alone, here—there are tons of mechanical devices put out to pasture as the ability to encode and decode messages advanced. The museum collects them all, from the first published book on cryptology (1518's *Polygraphiae*) to devices used by Thomas Jefferson, including once-secret military encryptors from the Civil War through to the Cold War. Aside from the large collection of artifacts dating to both world wars, there's a room devoted to giant old computers, like the purple-shelled Zeigler, made by Cray Research and nicknamed "Barney" after the kid's show host. That nickname is quite appropriate, as it turns out, because now the machine really is a purple dinosaur! Nearby, a StorageTek Automated Cartridge System stays busy, as a tall robotic arm hussles around a central cylinder of computer tapes, grabbing them with a lighted fist and slotting them into the opposite wall. Ingram assures me it's not doing real work. "It's just a library system," he notes. "We just have enough tapes to make it work, but it will do 450 different centers an hour." So you needn't worry that it's recording your roommate's hacking activities, I mean instant messages, while you're enjoying the museum!

The really eerie stuff is the most modern, found in the last room. Among the analog disk cipher wheels and dozens of devices to secure radio transmissions during past wars lie more modern computerized biometric authentication and recognition equipment that can peep you, sniff you, and read your palm. If this stuff is declassified, what's currently hidden in the back room?

The displays are not all sinister gadgets and humorless history. Thick code books also share the space, one which translates messages into line drawings of women's clothing. Shades of *Get Smart*'s shoe phone! Seeking more (unintentional) comic relief? Look no further than America's first intelligence satellite, a spiky silver ball looking smart and radiant—in a 1960s way.

On a recent visit, I was greeted at the door by three exhibit cases full of cryptologic toys from the Golden Age of Radio to the 1980s. It doesn't matter if you don't remember the Secret Squadron, Captain Midnight, or Radio Orphan Annie's Secret Society; these club pamphlets, code books, and metal badges comprise a cool pop subculture. There are also gadgets from Dick Tracy, Indiana Jones, and James Bond. Looking for other necessary spy gear? Check out the Tom Mix Six-Gun Brass Decoder Badge, with a little pistol that spins to different symbols, and the "Secret Agent" lunch box and thermos.

It's nice to know this stuff has been declassified for museum display. Actually, these toys are on temporary loan from collector Richard Brisson, Ingram says: "They'll probably go back to the owner when I retire." Be sure to see them soon.

National Firearms Museum

National Rifle Association Headquarters Building
11250 Waples Mill Road
Fairfax, VA
(703) 267-1600
Website: www.nra.nationalfirearms.museum
Hours: Open daily 10 a.m.-4 p.m.
Cost: Free

If there was a Midas-like king whose touch turned everything into a gun, he'd open a museum like the National Firearms Museum (NFA), which purports to show the role of firearms in the development of America—but it's really just an excuse to look at lots and lots of guns! Old, historic, decorative, manly guns. Some owned by Teddy Roosevelt, Buffalo Bill, Annie Oakley, and even Charles Manson! How many guns would you like to see? OK, so they *only* have "more than 2,000" on display, and it's *only* the largest collection east of the Mississippi. However, it is the world's most diverse collection, covering civilian and military firearms, plus ammunition and accessories.

The curators have spread this loot across fourteen galleries, each focusing on a different aspect of American history. Well, just the history that involves, uh, guns. Like the American Revolution, western expansion, Civil War, Spanish American War, and the two world wars, through Korea, Vietnam, and the first Gulf War. Each area centers around a life-size diorama, featuring mannequins with guns. In the model of Teddy Roosevelt's luxurious Long Island home, a giant fiberglass rhino's head stares you down as a bookcase fades away and a wall of sporting guns appears! There are GIs chilling in a shelled-out Nazi hideout, moments after scrawling "Kilroy was here" on the wall. Meanwhile, the doughboys manning a Marlin machine gun in a trench on the Hindenburg Line (1918) seem to be having a little less fun. These exhibits emphasize the great advancements in weapons technology required by each conflict. Naturally, they're accompanied by lots of historic examples of guns both big and small, representing all different models and gauges.

As the galleries aren't laid out consecutively, it's easy to lose track of where you're supposed to go next. It doesn't help that the areas all look pretty much the same: just glass cabinets full of guns. Whether you're checking out hunting rifles, BB guns, long rifles, or contemporary models, the stories behind these artifacts are often lost. The excitement of the

"Frontier Justice" display is reduced to a few photographs and lots of tiny pistols arranged on a wall. But there are some nice souvenirs from Annie Oakley and Buffalo Bill: pistols, naturally, but also a small card with Oakley's signature and a real bullet hole through a printed heart. These pop culture rarities make the museum's collection shine—especially for those who know nothing about firearms of any type.

If you do know a rifle from a shotgun, however, you'll notice that the NFA owns one of each type that once belonged to Oakley. "She used a little bit of everything," notes museum curator Doug Wickland. "She used handguns as well as long arms. Her favorite rifle that we have is a Remington 32. It takes a 32 rimfire cartridge. It was a single shot gun that you open up to load, then you pull out the spent case and put another one in. It was very labor intensive; just one shot for all that activity." Oakley also tested her talents with the "little 410 shotgun" in the case next to the rifle.

Many displays emphasize the craftsmanship of these weapons. That's particularly justifiable with the older pieces, where intricate carvings; inlays of pearl, bone, ivory, or metal; gold damascening; or cast silver parts are so finely done that the pieces are clearly works of art. Two beautiful rifles feature tiny, carved ivory inlays depicting lion, deer, fowl, and other game animals. It's a long way from here to the mass-produced guns of mass destruction used in the French trenches, further still to the modern weapons surrounded by posters of "America's Most Wanted." The curators are careful to stay away from these heavy messages, focusing instead on firearms as tools of defense and liberty, or of sport and amusement.

The selection of modern weapons is so vast it's easy to get lost in it, even when using the computerized catalog. Some interesting pieces pop up, including a miniature Colt single-action Army pistol, complete with holster and saddle, on loan from Charlton Heston. "I'm not sure finding ammo for it would be as easy as some of the other pieces that he loaned us," Wickland deadpans, referring to the real guns Heston sent for the museum's "Real Guns of Real Heroes" exhibit of 2002. That show also included Dirty Harry's Smith & Wesson double action revolver, alongside his police badge; these items are still at the museum, on extended loan from John Milius, the screenwriter for both *Dirty Harry* and *Magnum Force*.

But the most surprising gun on display has to be the Winchester shotgun once owned by Charles Manson. Wickland is ready with the details on the piece. "It was basically a shotgun that was sold by the U.S. Military as surplus after World War II. After that we can't really track it down, but then it turned up in [Manson's] hands, and it was confiscated from him," he explains. "This is well before he did anything up around Hollywood."

Next, the shotgun went to an agent at the California Department of Fish and Game. "They were pretty shorthanded when it came to materials," Wickland reveals, "and it was a good shotgun, so they kept it in service." Nonetheless, the department gave the agent the gun when he retired; he, in turn, gifted it to the museum. Imagine the crazy movie treatments that could come out of that story!

One might suppose it's extraordinary for a privately held, specialized museum to have so many generous and big name friends, but the National Firearms Museum isn't just a mom and pop operation. It's actually an educational project of the National Rifle Association, founded back in 1937 when the NRA had its headquarters in Washington. "We basically tell the story of firearms, freedom, and the American experience," Wickland says. "We tell the story of Americans and their guns." In 1993, the NRA closed to move into the new office tower it built for itself along Route 50 in Fairfax, Virginia, reopening its operations gradually, starting in January 1994.

While the museum waited for its own space to open in the new building, Wickland assembled smaller shows on the second and fourth floors. The NFA's grand reopening in 1998 showed it had become a major museum. "We're about six times the size of what we were in Washington, DC," Wickland notes. "[Back then] we had perhaps 600 to 700 pieces on display; now, over 2,000 pieces are represented." In addition to maintaining the museum exhibits, the curatorial staff also mounts displays for gun shows and presents special programs, like the one they gave at the Lewis and Clark Bicentennial celebration.

Although some might lament the way the museum seems to glorify gun evolution during history's darkest hours, anyone would forgive these excesses once they arrive at the loving replica of a classic 1950s boy's room. Marvel at the mint-condition Hopalong Cassidy linoleum on the floor, ranch style wallpaper, and the delightful chenille bedspread decorated with a colorful cowboy waving from his galloping horse. The treasures are simply too numerous to list: coonskin cap, covered wagon lamp, LPs, books, and more. Not just a fortune on Ebay, but a time capsule of pop culture dreams. In a small glass case along the front of the display there are air guns and cap guns galore, and in another nearby case, the first Daisy BB gun. "We went to many different antique shops in order to outfit that room," Wickland says. "And many members of staff also contributed items from their childhood. One of the pictures that's on the mirror there belongs to our membership director. It has him in a cowboy outfit; I think he was eight or nine years old at the time."

Cross the hallway of the gallery where these nostalgic wonders reside and the 1903 Coney Island shooting gallery rolls into action as you approach. It lives! A large wheel with targets shaped like diamonds, spades, and other card insignia revolves, a row of ducks waddles across the bottom, and a line of squirrels climbs the sides. A flock of little birds just waits to be picked off. It's another piece of Americana the Smithsonian might not dare to show.

If that shooting gallery could talk, it could tell some amazing stories. Wickland relates that it was manufactured at Coney Island and was originally powered by steam. Sometime in the 1920s it would have been converted to electricity. After thousands of people fired at it over the decades, it was replaced—possibly in the 1940s or 1950s. "It might have gone on a tour through state fairs, or it might have been put in a different location," Wickland guesses. What's certain is that a very lucky Ohio man acquired it as the centerpiece for a private shooting gallery. He actually fired on it for a few years before packing it away in his barn, Wickland says. After storing it for a few decades, the man donated it to the museum.

The curators must have wondered if the shooting gallery was worth the trouble. First of all, it was made of iron and steel plates, so it was "very, very heavy," Wickland notes. "Just amazing how much weight's represented in something that looks basically two dimensional." The thing must have looked a sight, too, because as the museum restored it, they removed "enough rust to fill a fifty-five gallon drum," he says. Stripping it down to the bare metal was only the beginning—it then needed paint. "The original colors were tough to determine," Wickland explains, "but we were able to establish what the original paint colors were. That's what the piece is painted."

Then came the installation. "It was a tight fit to put it into the allocated space that we had," Wickland remembers. "It was broken down into many, many pieces for transportation. As we put it back together in the museum gallery, it took quite a bit of swearing and contortion, but it does look nice, and it is fully functional."

Don't even ask if you can take a shot at it, though. "With all the glass in that particular gallery, the danger of ricochet would be too much," Wickland says drily, adding quickly, "But before the glass was installed it was fired on one last time just to make sure everything was fully functional."

As a consolation, trigger-happy visitors can use the NRA firing range, also in the building. There are two catches, however: The targets don't turn, and you have to bring your own gun.

National Glamour Archives

Alexandria, VA
Website: www.hometown.aol.com/amsiea/index.html
Hours: By appointment only;
contact Art Amsie by email at amsiea@shentel.net
Cost: Free

The view of the Potomac River from Art Amsie's high rise condo in Old Town Alexandria, Virginia, is spectacular, but I don't really notice. My eyes are glued to the wall of original pin-up paintings rendered for calendars during the 1940s to the 1960s by artists like Gil Elvgren, Ed Runci, Fritz Willis, Joyce Ballantyne, Alberto Vargas, and Ed d'Ancona. The subjects are all women with killer curves, dressed out in bright, form-enhancing clothes. You see naughtier stuff in today's Victoria's Secret catalog, on television, in mainstream magazines, but back in the day, cheap reproductions of these paintings defined a male's private domain of the garage, the den, the workbench. "Pin-ups transcend mere eroticism," Amsie says, by way of offering a definition. "They may be interpreted as being subtly erotic. They're aesthetically arousing."

Amsie's always ready to extemporize a lecture on his favorite subject, even when we're just setting up a phone interview. "This whole concept of pin-up is a very dynamic thing," Amsie begins without warning. "Sex has been fundamental since the dawn of mankind. In the field of sex there's all sorts of grades, classes, and levels of respectability. Sex is a part of marriage, to have children; sex is used for entertainment, that's the guys who are bar hopping. A well-delivered, well-executed pin-up illustration is quite acceptable, and it reflects mankind in its entirety. If it's done coarsely, it's unacceptable. The pin-up calls to mind the togetherness of man and woman."

It's time, then, to distinguish pin-up from the other erotica, namely porno. "Men don't masturbate to pin-up," Amsie insists. "They may masturbate to a centerfold in Playboy or Hustler, or a Victoria's Secret catalog. But they don't masturbate to pin-ups. The pin-up transcends mere eroticism. Is perfume erotic? Not per se. Is lipstick and eyeshadow and other things girls put on to make themselves prettier—is that erotic? I guess if you have a great affinity for girls with rich red lips, yes. But in itself, lipstick and makeup and perfume, jewelry, sexy dangly earrings—all these things could be fetishes for individual people."

"I'm convinced that the pin-up is not pornography," Amsie continues. "It's become a crusade for me. I want the pin-up to be appreciated as a work of art—the way they should be. I'm an evangelist for pin-ups. I preach the gospel of pin-ups."

Mention pin-up around Art Amsie and you're sure to get a sermon on the subject. If you happen to be writing an article, you've got to be ready to write when he picks up the phone. Art has big ambitions—for me. "I want to help you become an effective documentarian of the pin-up," he tells me at one point. But he adds, "Are you calling long distance? I'm playing *Family Feud* here." He pauses to mumble answers to the televised game's questions.

A dynamic septuagenarian, Amsie's really from another time—a time when men were men, "and women do things to make themselves attractive, to interest someone." At our first meeting, Amsie settles into his chair, chomping a cigar and regaling me with anecdotes about being the only person in the world who knew and was friends with the Big Three of pin-up culture: cartoonist Bill Ward, painter Gil Elvgren, and model Bettie Page. If Amsie's dressed, uh, a little too casually to greet visitors formally, he's still king of his cluttered bachelor pad, a weekend HQ he shares with his son. His collection of original pin-up art fills one large wall. You can buy one for as little as two grand, but for an Elvgren, the creme de la creme, values start at $25,000. It's the Rat Pack version of retirement. The high life may not be so grand now, but Amsie's fish stories aren't about the ones that got away. Amsie is one of the trophy winners. He may be a big talker, but his stories are genuine—and he's right: everyone wants to know more about pin-up and Bettie Page.

As a photographer's model, Page certainly contributed to the social revolutions of sexual liberation and feminism. Bettie reigned over the 1950s pin-up scene, her dark bangs and pleasant smile giving a campy tone to all her pictures, particularly softening the most extreme fetish scenes smut photographer and peddler Irving Klaw could conjure. Spankings, bondage and discipline, leather and rubber costumes—Page frolicked through it all, managing to look both innocent and like she was having the time of her life. If the titillation seems tame by today's standards—Klaw often dressed her in two or three pairs of underwear to dodge censorship—the power of her image burns ever brightly. In December 1957, Page walked away from modeling and disappeared, making no appearances, no interviews, no photographs since. This could have been a great career move—death without dying—except Page never owned any rights to the images she helped create. Bettie Page may be penniless and isolated, but the classic images of her strength, beauty, and joyous eroticism have inspired women—and of course men—in increasing numbers. As a result, you can find her images on merchandise ranging from refrigerator magnets to comic books. And her story makes great TV and magazine fodder. It's the classic rip-off that happens to artists when they can't predict the influence of their work.

Late in her career, Page posed for "camera clubs"—amateur photographers, like Amsie, who would go out together on organized "Sunday excursions" to expose some film and a little flesh. As Amsie recalls, "You didn't join the camera club. Anybody could just walk off the street and pay the amount to go on the Sunday excursions. The Sunday excursions were two-fold: to get new potential customers for the camera club, and to introduce amateur models. Girls who wanted to be models would go out on a lazy Sunday afternoon and pose for the guys, hoping their work was acceptable enough that they'd be asked back to the owner's studio. The owner wanted to be the modeling agency—I don't want to say pimp—he wanted them in his stable. A lot of the guys would say, 'give me your address, and when I can go out I'll call you.' He'd take her out to his own studio or on location, and Cass Carr would lose the rent he'd charge for a few hours of his studio. So the girls were not supposed to give out their names or phone numbers. He'd tell the girls to come over and pose for nothing. The stars would get paid—like Bettie Page, Lynn Michaels, Judy O'Day, Mary Tress, Mary Troy. Because most of the photographers knew the well-known models: 'Oh, Judy O'Day's going to be there, she's great.' So she would go out and four or five more amateurs would go out."

As a camera club photographer from 1956 to 1957, Amsie happens to have produced some of the greatest camera club images of Page ever. He distinguishes his efforts as a photographer from those of the snapshooters in the world, but boils his skills down to one formula: "The magic word C: composition." It might have helped that he was perfectly willing to humble himself for a good shot, too—but only when working with the amateur models. "I'd have to tell the girls what pose I wanted," he explains. "Sometimes I'd get down and do the pose myself. Kneel down and sit back on your heels, hold your hands up and do this..."

And then there was Bettie. "Posing for me she sparkled, she effervesced, she scintillated, she glowed, she radiated," Amsie effuses. "She was so cooperative, it was incredible. The work that I did with Bettie, she was a true pro. She worked out the ideas that I wanted. When I wanted a particular pose, she knew inherently what type I would want. I would want pert, or haughty, or saucy, or tempting, effervescent. She could do that."

In other words, Page intuitively understood Amsie's original formula for the perfect pin-up: "pose, clothes, and expression." Amsie recites this mantra like he's relishing a good whiskey, rolling each word carefully over his tongue. It's what everybody sees when they look at an Elvgren, but not everyone can identify what's giving the picture its zing.

Amsie's photographic legacy may come down to two pictures he produced by accident, at the end of a day of shooting, with two frames left on a roll of film he just wanted to finish. Perhaps it was Amsie's special rapport with Page that kept them together on the boat ride back to their cars, and her willingness to do a couple more shots.

"It's only in retrospect that I realized that of all the other recent photographs, there are no other candids of Bettie," Amsie notes, still with awe. "Talk about falling into a dumb luck. And it turns out that's the most popular—I've sold hundreds of that picture where she's holding her hands up and her blouse is blowing open." And there she is, the girl next door with a silk scarf tied around her head. Her trademark black bangs cover her forehead; the smile is genuine, her blue eyes friendly. Somehow, the top two or three buttons of her red blouse with white polkadots never got fastened, and a plain white bra like your sister would wear reveals itself to the camera. A woman in cat glasses sitting behind Page looks over to see what's up.

"When I had the second shot," Amsie continues, "I said, let's do something funny. Take this fender and act like it's a great big sausage, or a submarine sandwich. Make like you're taking a bite out of it." This time, Page's blouse is chastely fastened. Her blue jeans are rolled up to just below the knee, and her red fingernail polish matches her blouse. Her open mouth hangs over a tubular plastic buoy. The shot may be silly, but it captures both the high spirits Page brought to her professional work as well as the country girl behind the scenes.

"Even a blind pig will find an apple," Amsie notes, for once showing some self-depreciation. Both photos usually make it into most books about Page's life, and they made the cover of *Betty Page: Private Girl*, a collection of "spicy music" played by a no-name strip club band and released by Germany's Normal Records. The deluxe digipak includes a generous portfolio of classic Page images. The label didn't pay Amsie for his work. ("I don't need the money," he says dismissively.) Instead, he took copies of the disc to sell through his archives.

Among his other accomplishments—a career in engineering, making a killing on the stock market, achieving National Master rank in tournament bridge—Amsie claims to have started a renaissance of pin-up when he opened his retail store Girl Whirl on King Street in Alexandria, Virginia.

It was 1976, "the height of the pornographic era," Amsie remembers. The *Washington Post* ran an article on the place in which a much younger Amsie boasted: "I stand alone, one with banner unfurled, against a tide of pornography, trying to bring Americans back to where they enjoyed beauty." After quoting himself during our interview, Amsie remarks that he's "patronizing the early Art Amsie," but he clearly holds on to his earlier ambition and hubris, declaring, "I wanted to be the leader of a movement."

Amsie called his shop the Girl Whirl "because people used to walk in and whirl around. They did a 360 because it was all over the walls, the paintings and illustrations and calendars." Mostly he sold low cost items, but occasionally someone bought one of the paintings he'd begun purchasing at trade shows and auctions. Although he'd been a lifelong collector of pin-up magazines and photos, starting at age thirteen, Amsie hadn't known he could buy paintings. But once he started, hundreds went through his hands as he sold some off to pay for the ones he wanted to keep.

Amsie ran the Girl Whirl until rising rents in 1983 drove him out of retail, at which point he established the National Glamour Archives as a home-based gallery to show, and sometimes sell items from his collection. Today, Amsie estimates he owns 150 original cartoons Bill Ward rendered for the digest-sized girlie rags of the 1950s and 1960s (*Zip, Breezy, Gaze, Laugh Riot*), plus enough cartoons by others to bring the collection of drawings to 200. He's got boxes of classic pin-up ephemera, including cards, magazines, stereo slides, and photos—plus originals of Bettie in bondage he bought at Klaw's shop. Of his 100 or so paintings, only the ones for sale are currently on display. Also on offer are prints of Amsie's Page shots and some Klaw pictures.

He defines the place as "a museum of classical pin-up and glamour illustrations holding the embodiment of feminine attraction. And a little bit of really innocent voyeurism, along with some humor." But there's really no museum here. It's not national at all—rather exclusive in fact, as far as public viewing goes, since you need an appointment to get in—although Amsie gets orders from all over the world. Most customers find him through the Internet (www.hometown.aol.com/amsiea/index.html). By his own admission, the National Glamour Archives intends to do justice to his collection. "This is for the glorification of Art Amsie," he says impishly. "This is a self-fulfilling effort." Which makes it a classic piece of local color—even though you have to dig for it.

Sometime in the mid-1970s, Amsie also became drinking buddies with master pin-up painter Gil Elvgren. "I've been a fan of his for sixty-two years," Amsie crows. "That's not older than you—that's older than your father!" To Amsie's mind, Elvgren created an iconic and often imitated pin-up image. "The women were not erotic," he explains. "They were as close to Shirley Temple as you can get in a mature atmosphere. They were sexy, but they were endearing, huggable, and sweet." Elvgren's prodigious output for Brown and Bigelow calendars helped create a new art form, as Amsie tells it.

"They didn't have pin-ups before the twentieth century," he lectures. "All paintings were either classical or pornographic. Whether you take the Kama Sutra, or some of the Japanese woodcuts showing orgies, things like that. Or you would have Botticelli's 'Birth of Venus,' or Aphrodite, or Nike. Then this whole concept of teasing and titillating came along." Amsie breaks off. He just can't resist adding, "Well, women have always teased men, haven't they?"

Amsie continues, "Pin-up definitely satisfies me emotionally and aesthetically. I have a great feeling for pin-up. I guess it's nostalgia, yes. I guess it was coincidental that the pin-up became very strong during the war years, when I was thirteen and fourteen. The soldiers and sailors would always have pin-ups. And they photographed pretty girls. And I liked pretty girls: I liked the way they looked, I liked the way they smelled. I saw the dictionary, it says 'pornography: that which tends to arouse sexually.' I think pin-up is far beyond that. Because a girl puts on perfume and it turns her boyfriend on. Is that pornographic because it tends to arouse sexually? I disagree with that. The people who did the Merriam-Webster must have been some goofballs. Sexy lingerie, a little lacy slip that a girl walks around in: is the slip itself pornographic? A little nylon and lace. Why is it important? It's a part of our culture, so it's a part of our history. It would be sufficient just from a historical standpoint, from World War II, since it helped to win the war. Which it really did, because it kept the morale of the troops up. But aesthetically, yes, definitely. It's a different type of subtle eroticism, arousability."

Later in our conversation, I'm able to goad Amsie a bit with a short, simple question: "Is pin-up sexist?" Amsie sputters, but gets down to the soundbite business. "There's at least two answers," he growls. "Yes, it is sexist—if the woman does not agree to it. But [not] if the woman agrees to the pin-up, and depending on how erotic the pin-up is. If a woman has nothing but beauty, she would be absolutely stupid not to use it! It would be like a guy who can shoot basketballs from fifty feet out, or a guy who can drive a golf ball 400 yards not playing golf! Now, if men try to use women who are not interested in that, and if they try to convince women who don't have a specific propensity for posing themselves, then that is sexist. Do some men use it for sexist purposes? I imagine so. But why do women go to Victoria's Secret to get sexy lingerie? The statement is absolutely ridiculous. You stepped into a hornet's nest with me, when they say sexist. I say go to hell! In fact, Bettie Page didn't mind doing nudes. She said 'I enjoy doing nudes because I'm proud of my body.'"

Amsie's attitude reflects a gentle chauvinism that matches the subtle eroticism of his collection, his life's work. Some may call him a cad, but really Amsie's a gentleman—one who respects women in their totality, but particularly what a gal can do with a little lipstick or lace to rock his world. That artfulness is the power of the pin-up. And it's the true *raison d'etre* of Amsie's archives.

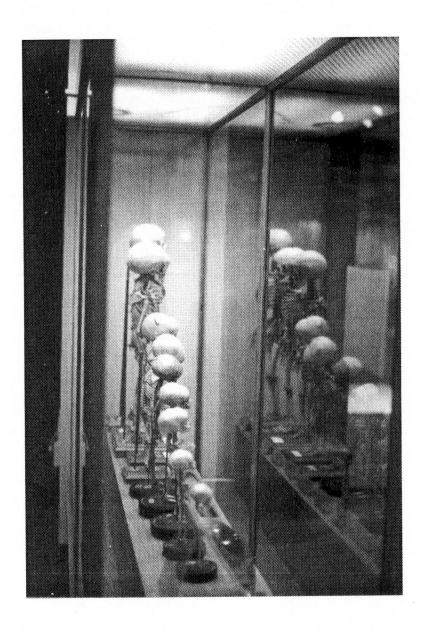

National Museum of Health and Medicine

6900 Georgia Avenue and Elder St., NW
AFIP, Building 54
(Walter Reed Army Medical Center)
Washington, DC
(202) 782-2200
Website: www.nmhm.washingtondc.museum
Hours: 10 a.m.-5:30 p.m. daily
Cost: Free

Step right up! See the cyclops baby! Witness for yourself the ravages of syphilis, arsenic, and war! Watch a skeleton grow from a twinkle in daddy's eye to the neighborhood menace! Tattoos! Iron Lungs! Hairballs! Naughty bits and surgical kits! All for one money! Reach deep down in your pockets, and if you come up with nothing....Welcome!

The National Museum of Health and Medicine (NMHM) features room after room of eye-popping and stomach-churning spectacle—like a medicine show crossed with a midway sideshow, only no annoying "talker" and real specimens. This place is so over-the-top, you may find yourself wishing they provided barf bags. Of course, it's all educational. Only you'll learn more than you ever wanted to know about so many things: reproduction and development; war injuries; disorders of the major organs; venereal disease; and the history of medical "science."

Take human reproduction and development, for example. No boring charts or rambling captions here. Examine, if you dare, the plasticized *real* human pelvic cross sections—both his and hers, naturally—naked as the day they were born, and even a little more so. You'll see all the internal workings just as they're diagrammed in health textbooks, only here it's in the flesh. Literally. Models and preserved specimens document the growth of the human fetus from a few weeks to birth. Just to make certain points clear, there's a line-up of real skeletons, from a tiny four month old fetus to a five year old child. Then you get to the "pickled punks," as the sideshow carnies used to say. That is, congenital deformities of the human fetus. Including sirenomelia (a "mermaid deformity"), conjoined twins, achondroplastic dwarfism (as a bonus, the skeleton of a female dwarf can be found in the endocrine display), cyclopia (that is, a cyclops, with one eye), and anencephaly (what's been called the "pinhead"). Did I mention these are real?

Exhibits rotate here, but the emphasis seems to be on extreme medical ailments. And the NMHM has models or real specimens of everything. Ever wanted to know what arsenic poisoning, frostbite, sulfuric acid, acne, coal mining, or eating your own hair could do to a body? If you answered "No," you're certainly in the wrong museum. Get thee to the Smithsonian!

The museum has undergone tremendous changes since Surgeon General William Hammond first established the Army Medical Museum in 1846. He wanted "to collect anatomical specimens as well as projectiles removed from wounds, together with reports of cases," with the purpose of improving Army doctors' understanding of wounds and healing. The sensationalistic element of the museum may not be intentional; however, Hammond modeled his collection after other nineteenth century natural history museums. P. T. Barnum happened to be running a very successful example in New York City at the time.

In 1887, the Army Medical Museum got its own prominent location in a striking red brick building on the corner of Independence & 7th Street, SW, in Washington, DC, on what's now the National Mall. For eighty years, the Army Medical Museum Building attracted legions of visitors. After World War II, the museum became a division of the Armed Forces Institute of Pathology (AFIP), based at the Walter Reed Army Medical Center's campus. But the museum stayed in its place until 1968, when the Independence Avenue building was torn down to make room for the Hirschhorn Museum. Then the medical collection joined the AFIP on the Walter Reed campus, its present location.

Given the museum's history, those display cases crammed with artifacts related to Civil War injuries are NEVER going away. You may not want to know what an iron ball will do to a man's face, leg bone, skull, or any other part of his body, but Major General Daniel E. Sickles didn't mind dropping by to visit his amputated right leg. The bones are still there, along with the cannonball that shattered them in 1863. If Sickles were alive today, he could take his leg bones home on a postcard! (You can learn about Sickles' ghostly visits to his DC townhouse on the Capital Hauntings Tour. See the article in this book.) Currently, these artifacts are supplemented by displays on war injuries from the Civil War to the Vietnam Conflict, plus a special focus on Korean War era Mobile Army Surgical Hospitals (MASH units to you Hawkeye fans). You've only heard that "war is hell." The reality is much worse.

Other areas of the museum could be used as a set for a 1950s science fiction movie, with Vincent Price stalking around the Model SC Iron Lung (from 1950), Electrostatic Generator (1890), old x-ray equipment, or first electron microscopes (a dozen of them, dating from 1938). The latter round out a truly excessive collection of a hundred or so antique microscopes.

There's so much to see here. Did you visit the brain and spinal cord in a glass jar? How about the Japanese medical models demonstrating Zen anatomical theory? The tattooed skin sample? Did you touch the real, plasticized stomach?

Didn't get enough? Drop by the gift shop for a museum catalog, or better yet a postcard or magnet featuring the giant ball of human hair removed from a girl's stomach. There's even a hairball coffee mug! It's a great way to to revisit the National Museum of Health and Medicine every morning!

O. Orkin Insect Zoo

Smithsonian Natural History Museum
10th and Constitution
Washington, DC
(202) 633-1000
Website: www.mnh.si.edu
Hours: 10 a.m.-5:30 p.m. daily
Cost: Free

Cleopatra's about to eat lunch, but she isn't sharing. Her guests—a crowd of school kids watching her from a polite circle—don't seem to mind. The menu is a single cricket, after all. Hardly enough to go around.

While the docent lectures on the tarantula's feeding habits, she digs Cleopatra out of her box to show her off. You'd think a tarantula would put up a fight, but she just cowers in the giant's hand. Tarantulas are actually rather shy, being extremely fragile creatures; it's easy to snap off a leg or cause a more serious injury. Or maybe Cleopatra's not feeling too spry today, considering that she's a senior citizen, at least 30 to 35 years old! Back in her box, the spider freezes in a corner. Not even the sight of the cricket rouses her. The children crowd in for a closer look while their teachers and parents grimace. But hey, a spider's got to eat, right? Twice a day, at 11:00 a.m. and 3:00 p.m., visitors get to witness it. Uh, should they want to.

You don't often come face to face with a Mexican red-kneed tarantula (that's *brachypelma smithi*, for the scientifically minded) like Cleopatra, let alone stare down a giant leaf insect or a coneheaded katydid. But these creepy crawlies are par for the course in the only living exhibition on the Mall's museum row. Stag beetles, grasshoppers, water bugs, leaf-cutter ants and dozens of other species (sixty-five in all) hold court behind glass terrariums safely set in the walls on the second floor of the Smithsonian Museum of Natural History. Possibly the smallest zoo in the world, it doesn't need much floor space to pack in the wonders. Kids especially run from bug to bug like they're at an amusement park. Just check out the ant farm full of honey pot ants: Uncle Milton has nothing on this. See those round honey-colored orbs hanging from the tunnel roofs? Those are actually specially adapted workers who gorge themselves on the nectar regurgitated by foragers, storing it in their own abdomens. That's just a small sampling of the incredible evidence of insect diversity here.

There's a simple reason this place is so fascinating, despite the general impression of insects as pests or disgusting monsters. "The thing is that everybody has an insect story," explains Nathan Erwin, Manager of the O. Orkin Insect Zoo. "Doesn't matter what it is. We are always in touch with insects, whether we live in apartment buildings, or in a suburban house, or out in a rural area."

Every creature in this miniature zoo has a story, too. "One of the stories in the rainforest area that we're trying to tell is that phenomenal nutrient cycling that goes on from the canopy of the rainforest down into the soil," Erwin continues. "And the leaf-cutter ants are an important part of that, by clipping biomass from the canopy, taking it underground, and growing fungus on it. Ultimately, that biomass is turned into fertilizer for the tree roots and sucked back up again."

Technically a zoo for arthropods—the larger class of animals that includes spiders, lobsters, and millipedes, as well as beetles, butterflies, and ants—the Insect Zoo first started telling bug stories in temporary summer exhibits (occupying the current museum space) in 1971 and 1972. These proved so popular that a permanent, full-time installation was developed, opening in August 1976.

This initial version remained on view until 1992, when it was moved to a temporary location while the main space was renovated. Finding federal funds to redesign the zoo proved difficult, until a private donor, the Orkin Pest Control Company, signed on with a half-million dollar donation that earned them the naming rights. The "O. Orkin" of the zoo's name is actually Otto Orkin, who nearly a century ago founded the pest control business that also bears his name. "So the exhibit is actually named after an individual," Erwin points out. The redesigned exhibit opened in September 1993 and has held up ever since with minor modifications.

In this newest version, the zoo is divided into five habitats, showcasing the different strategies that insects and their cousins have used to adapt to their environments. Just by walking around, you can make quick visits to crabs, lubber grasshoppers, and giant walking sticks. One of the first things you'll notice is the giant model termite mound stretching from floor to ceiling in the main room. Those aren't giant termites you see crawling through the tunnel—they're just other people's kids swarming the mound.

At the pond habitat, you can play an aquatic version of "I Spy" by searching for water skimmers (on the surface) and giant water beetles (hanging upside down underwater with a breathing tube connecting them to air). The water boatmen are especially fun to spot—they're the sleek black beetles carrying a bubble of air as they dive to the bottom. The desert habitat showcases two kinds of scorpions (one is the vinegaroon, so named because it can squirt a vinegar solution from its tail), beetles, a huge centipede, and a tarantula—separated by glass partitions, of course.

In the far corner, there's a model house with a mechanized dog scratching lighted "fleas." Could they mean your house? Yes, indeed, it's another habitat, frequented by all kinds of nasty critters: silverfish, cockroaches, clothes moths, carpenter ants, the whole creepy crawly gang. Only here, you're visiting them. Um, can I donate my own "house guests" to the museum? "Our volunteers from time to time will help us restock with silverfish," Erwin admits, adding with a laugh, "But I will not put out an all-points bulletin for all the silverfish in the Washington area. I might be inundated!"

On the wall opposite the cutaway house, there's a window looking into another unlikely insect habitat: an entomologist's lab. It's a behind-the-scenes look at the zoo's stockroom, filled with shelves of plastic boxes and aquarium tanks with breeding populations used to resupply the displays. "A lot of people don't realize that less than fifty percent of the building is actually exhibit space," Erwin says. "There are giant collections behind the scenes where researchers are discovering new species of insects, understanding their relationships and interactions with other insect groups and ecosystems in general."

This lab area is the control center for zoo maintenance, too. But don't think the job's easy just because the space and its critters are small. "It's just like a large zoo, except we just don't take up as much space," Erwin explains. "Someone has to be here 365 days a year, just as they would at a zoo for large animals...They need to be fed, watered, exhibit cases cleaned, maybe eggs transferred, young taken care of, sometimes shipments received of new material from producers or suppliers. We maintain as many colonies as we can, so we don't have to go out collecting a lot or purchasing a lot." One thing they're not breeding in the back is red-kneed tarantulas. "We don't have the staff or the space," Erwin laments. "A female produces a fertile clutch of eggs, and you're dealing with 400 hatchlings. Then you have to put them in separate containers or they'll eat each other."

From outside the lab window, you won't have to worry about caretaking chores. You'll be too busy noticing the jars of soon-to-hatch black widow eggs, or the tank of giant hissing cockroaches, conveniently located to attract crowds of school kids and their groaning parents. These large, flat cockroaches are a big draw, especially when the interpreters bring them out for a viewing. Those who can stand it can even hold the things!

The interpreters frequently roam through the exhibit space with carts full of live bugs and their discarded exoskeletons, among other stuff for understanding arthropods. These close-up encounters are another big bonus of this little zoo, Erwin points out. "You can't get up and pet the elephant or the giraffe or the rhinoceros," he notes, "but you can hold a hissing cockroach, or a horn worm caterpillar, or a lubber grasshopper."

I'm always disappointed by the small "cave area," located in the rainforest zone, because I've never seen anything living in it. But Erwin assures me that there are indeed weird creatures called amblypygids, or tailless whip scorpions, living there. These spider-like creatures have extremely long front legs that Erwin describes as "buggy whips," which they use to detect food. One day I hope to see one. "They're tough," he admits. "Sometimes they hide around some of the stalactites that are hanging down. It's always a challenge."

Otherwise, the rainforest habitat is the zoo's *piece de resistance*, featuring a mysteriously darkened tunnel simulating the jungle floor, with a giant tree reaching into the high ceiling. Brush aside fake foliage to view a leaf-cutter ant farm wedged between the fiberglass tree roots. Smaller tanks hold butterflies, more stick insects, a stag beetle—and a large winged insect with a giant, striped, hippo-like head. It turns out this "coneheaded katydid" doesn't just look weird; it has unusual habits, too. "Until I started working here," Erwin says, "I've always thought of katydids as herbivores. However, the larger ones will eat both plant material and small insects. So we feed them crickets. Actually a combination of the two—some lettuce, or they sometimes nibble on the bromeliads we have in the case, or a little slice of apple."

The coneheaded katydid is a native of the Costa Rican jungle, but Erwin doesn't have to go stomping around in the tropical heat to round them up. Instead, the insects are raised on a butterfly farm in their native land and purchased by mail. Erwin notes that as the zoo's collection has moved toward more exotic insects, he prefers to buy them from specialized breeders in their country of origin. Such a plan demonstrates his commitment to a conservation ethic. First, he's avoiding the expense and uncertainty of a collecting expedition, and second, he's not removing material from the wild. Third and most importantly, he's supporting a legitimate business authorized and regulated by the Costa Rican government that is invested in preserving the country's rainforests. Erwin explains, "In order to maintain the butterfly farming and the farming of these other insects, you have to have areas you can take parent material from. In other words, you have to have intact forests there. So that's another way of promoting a conservation ethic, and providing an income for people who live in and near those forests."

Through its exhibits and its practices, the zoo reveals how humans and insects are inextricably linked. "Insects affect our lives in so many ways," Erwin explains, "whether they're producing honey or pollinating crops, or they're decomposing and recycling nutrients which...make those ecosystems run—forest, field, pond, stream, swamp, marsh. Without those insects, our ecosystems would come to a screeching halt."

So it turns out it's actually the bugs' world and we're just living in it. A visit to the Orkin Insect Zoo can help us understand our place here among them.

Pinck Room

Millennium Arts Center
65 I St., SW
Washington, DC
(202) 544-1343
Website: www.millenniumartscenter.org/index.html
Hours: By appointment only
Cost: Free

Noche Crist always wanted to start a brothel, so when her permanent art installation, the Pinck Room, opened at the Millennium Arts Center, she suggested that this fantasy boudoir be rented by the hour—but not for sleeping. Crist's friend, fellow artist, and Pinck Room curator/caretaker Judy Jashinsky recalls Noche plotting her whorehouse business and saying, "This can be the first room, and when we're successful, we can take over the whole hallway."

It's indeed an arousing space, complete with a bed, a bathroom, and the bidet Noche brought with her from Romania nearly seventy years ago. [Yes, you read that correctly. When the Pinck Room opened on May 24, 2001, Crist was ninety-two years old! Sadly, Noche Crist died on May 17, 2004, as this article was being prepared.] The walls are painted "clitoris pink." There's a cigar box filled with the tin caps from bottles of Veuve Cliquot champagne (Noche's favorite brand) consumed on premises—usually by the artist herself. Feather boas, feathered masks, satin ribbons, costume jewelry necklaces, and handcuffs lie around, in case you feel the need to dress up. Displayed throughout is a generous sampling from her library of erotic art books and vintage 1960s *Playboy* magazines. The added letter "c" in the installation's name is merely Crist's device to give the Pinck Room an exotic, East European feeling.

The Pinck Room's focus may be the bed covered with a purple blanket, but when you're alone in the place, the greatest fascination lies on the walls, hung with self-taught artist Crist's erotic paintings, drawings, and sculpture completed over the past three decades. Most of the paintings feature voluptuous, naked nymphs and weird hybrid beasts romping in stark landscapes. Over the bathroom door, there's a portrait of her mother, Juliet, reclining in a stuffed leopard print armchair and wearing a sheer, patterned body stocking; the painting is done on a plywood panel cut in the exact outline of the subject. Above the closed doors of the kitchenette, an odalisque reclines on an old-fashioned couch. Over the room's entrance, a large-busted, bat-winged harpy (a sculpture made of plaster) leans into the room. And there's a four-panel screen with portraits of provocatively dressed courtesans—the last being a self-portrait of the artist in a leopard skin cat suit! A place like this makes sense for an artist who made a career drawing, painting, and throwing parties, all relying on the sensuality of women's private spaces for their inspiration.

Who would have thought the boudoir of a nonagenarian woman could be so wild? Clearly, you've never imagined anyone like Noche Crist. Born and raised in Bucharest, Romania, Crist came to the U.S. after World War II on the arm of an Air Force officer who later joined the CIA. As a beautiful, exotic war bride, she was full of stories of her strange, sensuous upbringing in an upper middle class family, raised by her pleasure-loving Aunt Moumoutz and her doting, playboy husband Uncle Goe. Crist's mother spent most of her time in Swiss sanitariums, recovering from tuberculosis—after exiling the man she married at age sixteen (Noche's father) long ago. According to Crist's self-published memoirs, she never saw other children, but spent her time drawing, making imaginary worlds for herself in the abandoned upper stories of the house they lived in, and listening to the adults gossip about their worldly affairs.

According to curator Jashinsky, the family lived to party: "They slept late, got up, and prepared for the next evening's fun." In a 1998 interview with *The Washington Review*, Crist recalled, "I think I had a sort of unusual life because I never had a childhood. I was with grown ups. I knew everything, I saw everything. I was an old little girl." In one early memory, her aunt had taken her to a party at a monastery. "I was lying in a bed in a cell and everyone threw their coats on top of me," Noche remembered. "And then a couple came and made love on top of me."

So psychoanalysts will find it easy to explain Crist's obsession with beds, bedrooms, and the beast with two backs. In any case, the Pinck Room is the last in a series of similar environments Crist has created over the years. At her 1995 Washington Project for the Arts (WPA) show, titled "Boudoirs and Lupanars," she installed a canopied bed and other courtesanal luxuries in one corner, creating a private space in the public exhibition hall. She called this installation "The Transylvanian Bride," an autobiographical reference to her own first, unhappy marriage to, yes, a man from Transylvania. The painted headboard from that installation survives in the Pinck Room, mounted behind a large wicker chair.

The place above the Pinck Room's double bed (for the record, a different one than that used at WPA) is reserved for another whimsical, if scary, reference to her first marriage. Called "Tango With Transylvanian Husband," this giant wooden cut out shows a bat creature engaged in a frenzied dance with a nude woman who has a cat's head and tail and wears long black stockings. Fangs bared and wings spread, the bat man dips his partner in a deep backbend. Passionate, violent, and weird, the image riffs on themes of raw sexuality, failed romance, aristocratic decadence, and the vampire lore of Crist's native land. Her other paintings are filled with similar images; every piece seems to portray a party or grand ball, often amid ruins or stark landscapes. Perhaps it's Crist's way of dealing with the destruction wrought on her homeland during the Second World War, or in a larger sense, learned from Bosch and Breugel, a way to forget mortality in fleeting pleasures.

Crist's more traditionally square-shaped paintings often tell fascinating autobiographical tales. "The Geese of Ograda" shows naked women— some with wolf heads—stomping grapes alongside dark green beasts with the heads of fish, lizards, or rams. The creatures pour wine in each others mouths, and some of the women are so drunk they must be supported by several of the beasts. The pale green landscape is barren, split by pink gashes; a giant tub for wine-making rises in the upper right corner. Along the bottom, three large white geese sprawl as if dead. A kind of play in pictures, the painting is based on a true story Noche recounts in notes to the installation: "...the geese began to eat the remains after the grape harvest. It was hot and fermentation happened quickly. The geese gorged themselves, became drunk, and eventually passed out. The peasants thought the geese had died so they dragged them off and plucked all their feathers. Eventually the geese began to wake up to find themselves nude!"

Above the wicker chair, a round painting called "The White Moon" shows a naked woman reclining in a fountain, surrounded by dancing demons and hybrid animals. "Noche always tells me that's me," Jashinsky recalls, laughing. "As I was first starting to get to know her, she convinced me to be in a performance she was doing for the WPA [1989's "The Decadent Child"], to play her Aunt Moumoutz. So this was essentially her Aunt Moumoutz, who said all she liked was pleasure. She died a morphine addict."

Just outside the Pinck Room, to the left of the entrance, is Crist's rendering of the brothel from Faulkner's novel *The Sanctuary*. To the right of the door, "Death and the Green Dress" tells another true story. A bored-looking flapper lies on an old couch in a Bucharest brothel, while a flock of angry whores taunt her. It seems the young woman wanted to visit the brothel to see the ways of the world, but the employees didn't appreciate her curiosity. In the painting, one whore steals the young woman's pearls as another flicks cigarette ash on her green dress. As the story goes, the gown caught fire and the young woman died. Her distraught husband died weeks later. Both paintings subtly advertise Crist's ambition for the Pinck Room to become a whorehouse itself.

A hidden treasure of DC's art scene kept far too well, Crist's work surfaced now and then over the years in gallery exhibitions, sparkling with a wit and *joi de vivre* rarely seen in Washington. It makes sense that she was self-taught, instructed at age five by her Uncle Goe to "never copy" other artists. Her art was best showcased in her own home, forming the backdrop to elaborate parties with themes straight out of her art work (one bacchanal was called "Satyrs and Nymphs"). The perfect preserve of this spirit, the Pinck Room feels like a celebration. Enter this magical space and you can hear the painted figures begging you to pop the cork on a bottle of bubbly.

Provisions Library: Resource Center for Activism and Arts

1611 Connecticut Ave., NW, 2nd Floor
Washington, DC
(202) 299-0460
Website: www.provisionslibrary.org
Hours: T-F 11 a.m.-9 p.m.; Sat & Sun 11 a.m.-4 p.m.
Cost: $5 suggested donation

Local libraries seem so stodgy and repressed that the last time you may have visited was when your term paper was due, or to grab the latest bestseller for some beach reading. You'd never suspect that *any* library could be a hotbed of countercultural thought—as well as a great place to check out an inspiring art exhibit, have a conversation, or relax with a cup of coffee and the underground press.

If that's the kind of thing you're looking for, it's time to step up to the Provisions Library. With its daring collection of books and magazines, stylishly modern reading room, and spacious main gallery of intriguing art exhibits themed on issues of social justice and creative action, it's an outpost of radical culture that will change your preconceived notions of what a library can be. They show movies, host lectures, and even have a game night! A trip to this remarkable library may be the most enjoyable consciousness-raising you'll ever experience.

But a library's just a library until you scan the stacks. Most visitors roam over to the reading area, where racks of magazines wait to tickle your brain. Here's a jaw-dropping assortment of radically chic rags: *Anarchy, Car Busters, Comics Journal, Vegetarian Journal, Earth First!, Raw Vision, Punk Planet*—everything from *Adbusters* to *Z* magazine. It's got world newspapers, too, should you need to keep up with the *Guardian Weekly* or *Indian Country Today*. Now that's an intense sampling of the alternative press on contemporary art, leftist politics, avant garde literature, punk and world music, and social activism. Despite all this heavy lifting, the Provisions Library ain't all work and no play: there's room on the shelf for *Mad* magazine, too!

The book selection is equally mind-blowing, particularly for those familiar with the underground media represented in the AK Press and Amok Books catalogs. Between the reference collection and the circulating books, they cover everything that's cool, radical, or extreme. Books on

Dada, Fluxus and performance art; Black radicals; alternative medicine; graffiti; comics; punk; science and technology criticism...There's no need to make a list; Rigoberta, the online catalog, has already done it. (It's named after Rigoberta Menchu Tum, the Guatemalan activist for the civil rights of her Quiche Mayan people who won 1992's Nobel Peace Prize. Geez, you didn't think they'd name the thing after Monty Python, did you?)

Using Rigoberta, you can search out over 3,000 book titles and 300 periodicals. Do they have Annie Sprinkle's *Post Porn Modernist*? Check. How about RE/Search's bible of tattooing and piercing, *Modern Primitives*? Check. Books by anti-capitalist guru Noam Chomsky? Sorry, nope. OK, just kidding! (There's at least a dozen.) Um, then how about British graffiti artist Banksy's little books documenting his pesky satirical stencils? Check! Clearly, all libraries weren't created equal.

The Provisions Library opened in November 2001 as the Resource Center for Activism and Arts in a small gallery space in Dupont Circle. Deciding that name was too long and the space was too small, the library was renamed (keeping the original moniker as a subtitle) and relocated in March 2003 to the current office space on the second floor of an historic townhouse, on top of a dynamic strip of restaurants and shops, and just a block from the Dupont Circle Metro station. Despite the changes, the library's mission remains constant, and it still serves as an "experimental outpost where the public [can] have access to alternative publications and other resources on social change." According to its website, anyway.

"The idea to grow the library was about honoring a traditional public library, which we view as the most democratic resource of any community," explains Del Hornbuckle, the Provisions Library's Director—and chief librarian. "So we want to honor the traditional public library but go a step beyond that, reimagining what that could be if we didn't have to engage in censorship, or worry about government funding that stifles certain things, certainly around collection development." They were also interested in changing the experience of the typical library. "When you go into a traditional public library, you don't connect with art; you certainly aren't surrounded by socially concerned artwork," Hornbuckle continues. "So when you come to Provisions Library, you've got alternative materials, and you're surrounded by socially concerned art. The idea there is to stimulate dialog and think about alternative means and ways of being, social change, personal and social transformation—but in a creative way."

Between the design of the space, the development of the collection, and the planning of its programs, the Provisions Library creates the kind of "third space" apart from work or home that's been lost in our culture, but which is preserved in England as the pub and in Latin America as the plaza.

That third space must be free of commercial pressures and the need to be productive or focused on a particular task, as well as being "totally about community-gathering and community-building," Hornbuckle notes. "If you're talking about personal and social transformation, there needs to be some personal work and personal reflection. Part of that is about creating a safe space. So if you're feeling like, 'Why am I the only anarchist in Washington, DC'—you're not the only anarchist. You not only can come to a safe space where you can probably meet other anarchists, but you can read about an overall history of that movement, and even what that term means. You have material here that can support you on that journey. It's really important that you have a place and a setting that encourages you to explore that."

If you don't happen to be an anarchist, don't worry. "The communities we support are really everybody," Hornbuckle assures me, even though it helps if you have an alternative point of view. The point is to be democratic to the maximum degree, which means opening things up to ideas and identities that aren't represented in other places. She continues: "The library itself, in terms of the collection, is really about culling and bringing together in one place hidden histories and silenced voices—certainly from communities of color, the global south, but also from multiple communities, or subaltern communities—those that have made a decision that they don't want to be part of the dominant culture."

And if you're not a reader, the Provisions Library can still help you explore and express "often forbidden and suppressed ideas"; question "authority structures in our every day lives and the destructive, harmful, and limiting realities that are presented as normal and inevitable"; and "strengthen the imagination and enactment of peaceful and popular resistance, revolutions, new paradigms and cultures of liberation"—as it says on their website. That rhetoric may sound idealistic, but the frequently changing exhibitions of socially engaged art in the Blue Room gallery space (which also doubles as an auditorium) makes it fairly easy to achieve. Plus there's a regular schedule of educational programs, films, lectures, and music.

The art shows are often the main attraction. One of the most popular shows so far, called "Illegal Art," collected works that infringed on the copyrights of various capitalist overlords, I mean, Big Corporations. Organized by *Stay Free!*, an underground magazine which examines the negative effects of media and advertising on our culture, the exhibit included a Mickey Mouse gas mask and plans for a series of "Fallen Rapper" Pez dispensers. Recent shows have taken a more solemn approach to social problems, like Yun-Fei Ji's series of large classical Chinese-style paintings; amid the craggy mountains and flowing waterways of the Chinese landscapes, you find skeletal figures, toxic waste dumps...and other evidence of environmental hazards and human suffering.

But even activists get tired of tramping the moral high ground, so the third Thursday of every month is "International Game Night," where visitors can challenge each other to a nice round of Scrabble, backgammon, or Trivial Pursuit, among other board and card games in the library's collection. "Board games are a really low-tech way of getting together," Hornbuckle notes, "and one of the best ways to make connections between people. Since we're international in scope, it was really important to get games from all over the world. I did a lot of searching and got games from Europe, Africa, and South America." If you don't feel like Monopoly or Uno, you can just watch the movie playing, or listen to some music.

It's easy to find and easy to connect with the Provisions Library and its provocative collection. They're "hidden in plain sight," as Hornbuckle puts it, maintaining an accessibly modern, well-lit space, beautifully designed and artfully furnished with inviting leather and upholstered armchairs and a big comfy couch. The library's content is wild—sure to make you question the truths and consequences of your life and ideas. But the most radical thing about the Provisions Library is that you'll be so comfortable that if you're not already, you may find yourself converted to radical thought.

Squished Penny Museum

LeDroit Park, Washington, DC
(202) 986-5644
Website: www.squished.com
Hours: By appointment only
Cost: Free

You already know what an elongated coin is, even if you think you don't. These are the special tourist trap souvenirs you make yourself with one of those funny coin-operated machines with visible gears (some you crank and some are automated) that will flatten and emboss your penny with the logo of the place you're visiting. Numismatists—coin collectors to you and me—call them "elongated coins." But Pete Morelewicz and Christine Henry call them "squished pennies," a name that should catch on not just because it's more visual. You see, Pete and Christine own and operate a little museum in their DC townhouse, the Squished Penny Museum, dedicated to this folksy art form that combines the all-American pastimes of hucksterism, advertising, consumerism, and collectibles.

One of the best things about this home museum is its generous hospitality. Pete and Christine welcomed me on their porch, brought me inside, and started a long conversation about squishing adventures before ushering me over to the display boards. At the Squished Penny Museum, personal treatment is Job One.

The pennies themselves are so tiny that Pete has a loupe at the ready. The embossed coins are fun to look at—their simple, kitschy pictures and slogans make them a deliriously happy kind of folk art. But it's more fun to hear the curators talk about their oldest squished penny (NOT their 1893 Columbian Exposition souvenir, which is actually a squished 1891 Liberty nickel, but their 1901 Pan American Expositions' Temple of Music commemorative), most unusual (arguably Seattle's Sylvester the Mummy), or most difficult scores (the Seattle Space Needle ones, when they couldn't afford to go up into the tower together). They made all the display boards themselves (so you know the pair love museums as much as squished pennies), incorporating 250 of the coins alongside fascinating postcards and pamphlets from tourist traps across the U.S. The ongoing "permanent" exhibition, "The Open Road: Touring America Today," highlights twenty-five attractions. The display includes visits to the Circus Museum of Sarasota, Florida; Natural Bridge, Virginia; and Cadiz, Kentucky: "Home of the Ham Festival." But best of all is the mermaid imprint on the souvenir penny from Weeki Wachee, Florida. There are also copper commemoratives to buildings, feats of engineering, towers, zoos and museums, natural sites, sentiments, and the open road.

If that's not enough to see, there's also a handsome wood-framed glass showcase loaded with other goodies. Here you'll find their oldest elongated coins and a special exhibition supplement featuring selected pennies embossed with U.S. presidents, rightly named "Oval Officers: Profiles in Copper." "We have seventy-two," Pete says enthusiastically, "and we culled it down to twenty on display. We only have one George Washington—he's crossing the Delaware. There are lots of Nixons—on both sides: that he was 'crucified by Congress' and others shouting 'get out!'"

The collection is constantly growing. In 1999, when I first visited the Squished Penny Museum, they had only 2,000 pennies. On a more recent visit, the collection had more than doubled to between 5,000 and 6,000. Lest this seem like untold wealth, they inform me that while defacing American currency this way is permitted by law, once a penny's squished, it's no longer legal tender. Donations, constant foraging, and trades have all helped expand their horde.

But the biggest additions to the museum have made a bigger impact on the collection. The pair now own a penny press and work with a coin engraver to make custom dies for themselves and others. People have made their own squished penny business cards, moving announcements, and wedding invitations. In fact, Pete recently asked Christine to marry him using a squished penny embossed with his proposal. That's not surprising for a couple so obsessed with penny lore that they bought thousands of uncirculated pennies from the "all copper" days before 1982. Pennies made after this date tend to streak when they're squished.

Another highlight is trading for pennies at their kitchen table—bring 'em if you've got 'em. Even if you come empty handed, you won't leave that way. Pete keeps a jar full of giveaways for younger visitors, as well as pennies especially stamped with the Squished Penny logo by their friend and fellow collector William Massey, president of the Elongated Collectors, an organization just for penny squishers. Visitors can even squish their own pennies on a couple different machines. Besides the penny press, there's an old souvenir machine from Fort Benning, Georgia, that prints four different designs. Pete loaded me up with samples, certain I'd be infected with the collecting bug. (He was right.) Be sure to ask for their list of places to find squished pennies in the DC area.

Pete and Christine are a wealth of knowledge on where to squish, the history of squishing, and how to get your own machine. Come prepared to trade squished pennies, but also tales of how they got that way, and how you got them. They're generous listeners, too.

Summer House

West Lawn of the Capitol grounds
near New Jersey Avenue, NW
Washington, DC
Website: www.aoc.gov/cc/grounds
/art_arch/summer_house.htm
Hours: Anytime
Cost: Free

One of Washington's most delightful architectural treasures is virtually unknown—even though it lies in the shadow of a nationally famous building, the symbol of the democratic republic.

I discovered the Summer House by accident. When I worked at Union Station, I used to walk down New Jersey Avenue onto the Capitol's West Front Lawn looking for a secluded place to eat lunch. The best spot turned out to be a hexagonal, one-story outbuilding made of brick that enclosed a small fountain. In the spring, after the blossoms fell from the nearby trees, bees would swarm the place. Once, in the summer, boys came by on their bicycles and climbed into the fountain to play in the water. Then there was the tour guide who came through, telling a couple that in the 1800s senators watered their horses there. I called it "The Chapel" because of the intimacy and beauty of this small space which opened on the sky and promoted quiet meditation—a relaxing retreat from the office.

Which is exactly what landscape architect Frederick Law Olmsted had in mind when he designed the structure as part of his extensive work on the Capitol grounds. Olmsted, who also designed New York's Central Park, wanted to create a "cool retreat" that would "sweeten the air with fragrant ivy" and delight the ear with the "musical murmurings" of the spring water he had piped into a hidden rock garden. Olmsted's "Summer House" was built between 1879 and 1880, fulfilling his Victorian ideas of tranquility and whimsy in contrast to the formal white marble of the gargantuan Capitol—but only partially.

"The only thing that didn't pan out were the 'musical murmurings,'" Bill Allen tells me. As Architectural Historian for the Office of the Architect of the Capitol, Allen is singularly able to clarify the mystery of this forgotten tower. "Olmsted intended there to be a water-powered carillon set in the rock garden," he continues. "One was made by Tiffany, but it didn't work. It was consigned to a warehouse, and no one's seen it in 120 years."

When I mention the anecdote of the senators' horses, Allen is skeptical. "It must have been a roguish senator," he remarks. "The fountain was never intended for that purpose. Horses were never intended to come onto the lawns." And perhaps with such roguish senators in mind, Olmsted designed the place "to be open enough so that it wouldn't be used for illicit purposes."

The Summer House is partially screened by hedges and other vegetation, but its red brick walls stand out rather boldly against the official surroundings. On closer inspection, the basket weave brickwork of the outer walls, broken by three elaborate door arches with fanciful spiral endpieces, announces that you're entering a world apart. The walls are set with three wide oval windows, each screened by an art noveau grating. Descending a small stairway to enter, you'll find these windows are framed by a scalloped slate border and flanked by niches shaped like a child's outline of a suburban tract house—square with a peaked roof—filled in with swirling, neo-Celtic patterns. Compounding the whimsy, each niche has a different pattern. Under the windows, rows of slate seats await, promising meditative rest for up to twenty-two pilgrims. These seats are sheltered by a slanted roof covered with curved terra-cotta Spanish tiles, forming a scalloped pattern to further soften the straight-laced surroundings and add to the fantastic feel of the place.

But the Summer House's greatest feature can't be seen from the outside, where a cluttered garden of shrubs and sea grass only hints at it. Once inside, you discover that one of the oval windows looks onto a miniature jungle waterfall, complete with hanging plants and moss. A faery garden without the faeries, the simplicity of this secret view consistently offers surprise and sustenance. On a hot summer day the scene can be especially magical and refreshing, like an aboveground Luray Caverns—which has lead many guidebooks to label the Summer House as the "Spring Grotto," or the "Capitol Grotto," if they mention it at all. That kind of neglect can be good. The Summer House is one secret that peace-and-quiet-seeking visitors may want to keep to themselves.

The Textile Museum

2320 S Street, NW
Washington, DC
(202) 667-0441
Website: www.textilemuseum.org
Hours: Mon-Sat 10 a.m.-5 p.m., Sun 1-5 p.m.
Cost: Free; suggested contribution of $5.00

Walk into a room lined with hanging rugs and cloth, and your fingers just beg to touch the colorful, fuzzy stuff. If you're in a department store, that's the idea—the soft texture of a shirt or jacket will help make a sale. But if you're in a museum, touching is a big no-no, since one's fingers will leave a damaging film of grease and acid on the rare, historical materials. A visit to the Textile Museum, in DC's Kalorama neighborhood, presents just such a dilemma for the hands—and it also offers a solution in its Textile Learning Center (TLC), which offers a room full of yarn and cloth from around the world to handle and experiment with.

The only museum of its kind in the U.S., the Textile Museum is so nutty about cloth that wall signs actually request that you "please understand the needs of the textiles," by way of explaining why the lights are dim, the rooms are cold, and your hands must stay in your pockets. Don't worry. Your eyes are in for a treat that's well worth these minor inconveniences.

The museum is serious because it has a lot to share—over 17,000 textiles, carpets, and textile-related objects dating from 3,000 B.C. to the present. Exhibits draw from this vast wealth to create delightful displays of color and pattern in two different galleries. A recent show in the Main Gallery featured nineteenth century Navajo blankets. These simple pieces of cloth are so bold in their design, they resemble modern works of abstract art. And the wall texts clearly and carefully describe the weaving techniques and social uses of each piece. Even those who aren't textile fans will find themselves fascinated. But there's more!

Upstairs in the Collections Gallery, exhibits change every six months, and generally echo the Main Gallery's focus, while demonstrating similar principles at work in different cultures. Paralleling the Navajo's use of blankets as outer garments, "Draped, Unwrapped and Folded: Untailored Clothing," showed how the cultures of Ghana, Madagascar, Bolivia, Bhutan, Burma—and many others—used untailored bolts of cloth to fashion clothing. Expect all the exhibits here to demonstrate a sensitivity to cultural diversity, clearly explain the social purpose and meaning of the garments, and discuss the techniques used to make them.

The Collections Gallery is actually paired with the Activity Gallery, also on the second floor, to form the Textile Learning Center. While the Activity Gallery offers hands-on exhibits of how weavers make different types of cloth, the Collections Gallery rotates displays demonstrating these principles in historic pieces. Together, the galleries explain how textiles are made, who makes them, and why they are important.

After visitors have kept their hands to themselves for so long, the Activity Center is likely to spoil kids of all ages—and their fingers—with samples of traditional materials from Bhutan, Indonesia, and the Mapuche Indians of the Chilean Andes that demonstrate the diversity of embroidery and weaving techniques. One of the more unusual materials is the Kuba cloth from central Africa, made from the palm-like leaves of the raffia plant. The display clearly shows how a foundation cloth is made using plain weave, the most basic structure woven on a loom, where warp (vertical) and weft (horizontal) yarns simply interlace. Then the weaver adds a pattern by cut-pile embroidery, which creates a raised, brush-like effect. Even though the pile is stiff, it's surprisingly soft. It's a joy to rub one's hands on this material—it feels like a massage with a soft brush.

Children as young as four will love running from station to station, fingering yarn, playing with the games, or making patterns with the stitching exhibit and the display of the Indonesian Ikat technique, where plastic strips are shifted to experiment with simple color patterns. Even if you're not a "textile freak," it's hard not to become enthusiastic about cloth when thumbing through twenty-four Plexiglas-encased samples of different structure-building techniques, from macrame to braiding and looping. Before you know it, you've built up an understanding of how textile folk artists use color, fiber, pattern, and structure as a kind of language to communicate aspects of their artistry, technical skill, and culture.

The museum is housed in two glorious neo-Classical mansions, one of them the former residence of museum founder George Hewitt Myers. Make time for a stroll down the boxwood-screened path of the backyard garden and around the spacious lawn. The back wall overlooks a dramatic drop down to R Street and a view of other Embassy Row properties. This comfortably shaded piece of paradise makes a quiet retreat from the city—a great place to park a non-textile-loving friend or partner.

Places That Are Gone

There are a few places that did not make it into this book—and not because they were too well known or weren't worthy, but because they are no more:

- Flora Gill Jacobs decided to close her Doll's House and Toy Museum on May 1, 2004, after twenty-nine years of business, auctioning off a portion of her collection of rare antique toys, dolls, and doll houses.

- The Nek Chand Fantasy Garden at the Capital Children's Museum closed in July 2004, as the museum itself shut down. These sculptures created by internationally recognized outsider artist Nek Chand offered a rare glimpse of the wonders at Chand's twenty-five acre sculpture garden in Chandigargh, India. After being removed from the CCM site, the sculptures will be restored, but only a fraction of them will be on display in the "new, improved" location for the Capital Children's Museum (scheduled for a 2008 opening).

- One DC restaurant that would have qualified for an article in this book was the Roma, on Connecticut Avenue. This traditional Italian restaurant didn't just serve wonderful food; it was filled with a circus's worth of taxidermied animals—tigers, wildebeasts, antelope, and many more—that founder Frank Abbo bagged on hunting expeditions in Africa. When the Roma closed in April 1997, the family auctioned off the stuffed animals and other restaurant paraphrenalia.

- Another Mondo eatery, the Honolulu, was a tiki restaurant in Alexandria, Virginia, that closed in April 2004 to make room for an expanded Beltway interchange. Run by David Chan, a former bartender at DC's old Trader Vics, and his wife Anna, the Honolulu was a perfectly preserved time capsule of tiki culture, dressed to the nines in beautiful rattan wall decorations, tabletop tiki lamps, wooden masks, and more Polynesian kitsch than you ever thought was available. The Chans served powerful mai tais and treated guests like family.

- The exhibits in the FBI's downtown DC headquarters were as amusingly strait-laced as those at the Drug Enforcement Agency Museum, but the FBI tour kicked things up a notch by ending with a shooting demo by a real agent! I love the smell of gunfire in the morning! One hopes the FBI tour will reopen once all the terrorism hysteria dies down. You can get tour updates on their website: www.fbi.gov/aboutus/tour/tour.htm.

- The Stabler-Leadbeater Apothecary Museum, in Alexandria, Virginia, is a literal time capsule. Once a working pharmacy that closed in 1933, it was left undisturbed, preserving medicinal specimens and practice in place since the nineteenth century when it was opened as a museum in 1939. The apothecary is scheduled to reopen after extensive renovations are completed. Check their website for more information: www.apothecarymuseum.org.

- I fondly remember visiting Storybook Land as a child, riding the go-karts and looking at giant fiberglass sculptures of Humpty Dumpty, Cinderella, Ali Baba's Cave, and other fairy tale characters. This children's amusement park in Prince William County, very near my hometown of Woodbridge, Virginia, closed in the early 1980s and long ago fell into disrepair. Someone probably built townhouses on the rubble.

- The Enchanted Forest in Ellicott City, Maryland, near Baltimore, was an equally grand fairytale wonderland that I never had the pleasure of visiting. The park lasted into the early 1990s, but eventually closed. Its exhibits are falling into disrepair, although Cinderella's coach was recently refurbished and sold at auction, and later on Ebay. The park's dragon still leans over the white castle entranceway, should you want to visit it at the Enchanted Forest Shopping Center.

- Finally, the Museum of Menstruation remains a legend among weird DC area museums, long after it closed in August 1998. I regret that I never visited it myself, although I did talk to proprietor Harry Finley by phone and encouraged him to reopen. Finley still hopes to establish a real MUM in a permanent location—one that is not his house. Meanwhile, he's created a virtual museum on the Web at www.mum.org. Check it out!

Each of these places was a huge inspiration to me as I explored Washington and wrote about its weird treasures over the years. I am forever grateful to them for enriching my life; they will be missed.

Contents by Subject

Use this list to locate mondo attractions by subject.

ZOOS

Printed in the United States
38216LVS00003B/37-42